JESUS

Who do you say He is?

Josh C. Jones

JESUS:
Who do you say He Is?

Josh C. Jones

JESUS
Who do you say He is?

by Josh C. Jones

This book is generously gifted to

____

By

____

Contents

Acknowledgment

"Trust in the Lord with all your heart, and do not lean on your own understanding. In all your ways acknowledge him, and he will make straight your paths."

Proverbs 3:5-6[1]

I would like to thank God first and foremost for His guiding Spirit on the creation of this book and all the material inside it. Without Him, I could not do anything. He is my strength, my rock, my firm foundation.

I would like to thank Brody Jespersen for creating his *Who Is Jesus?* group study for churches. Without this, I would not have had the opportunity to lead one of the small groups at my church—The Assembly of God—on this wonderful journey to learn more about and to overflow with Jesus. The group study at my church was called "Overflow With Jesus," and I like that title, so I use that saying in the book.

Through my time leading this group, I was offered the opportunity (okay, I seized upon the opportunity without actually asking about it—I know, I should ask, but there has been so much that I've learned about the Bible and Jesus throughout my journey that I had that burning desire to share what I had learned and what I believed he had revealed to me, and this was the perfect opportunity) to create my own teachings (sermon, PowerPoint, guides, etc.) based on the topics in this group study each week and to present them to all the members of my small group. I was able to add my voice to the teaching, and if you've read my other books, listened to my podcast, or read my blogs, then you know there would be common interpretations, deep inflection, retrospection, and, of course laughs. I don't always make the correct choice to fully trust in the Lord without leaning heavily on my own understanding, but this was definitely one of those times when I did, and I am so thankful for God with what he did.

It was through this learning experience that the Holy Spirit led me to create, not just in my own perception, but in the entire group's perception, such an engaging, informative, and commanding lesson which tied together very well with each week's topic; and I believe it was this leading that helped usher in a powerful move of the Holy Spirit in our group sessions. It was through my group member's good words and encouragement, and the prompting of God, that I sat down and compiled my teachings from that group study into this book. I do repeat three important points in the chapter "Jesus Our Healer," which Brody said in his video for that week. I felt they were too valuable to leave out of this book—another reason for Churches to incorporate Brody Jespersen's *Who Is Jesus?* into their group studies.

I encourage anyone reading this book to talk with their church about implementing Brody Jespersen's *Who Is Jesus?* small group study. There is a group discussion workbook that goes with this study of his. I believe it will be invaluable to the Church body. The videos can be found, by your church, at www. rightnowmedia.org.

I thank everyone who took a chance on me and joined me in that small group. It was God who inspired me to sign up to lead that group and to prepare my own lessons each week, but it was you who kept encouraging me week after week. I thank each and every one of you.

Chapter 1:

Prologue

"Every choice you make has an end result."

Zig Ziglar[1]

Thank you for your interest in this book, and your interest in getting to know and understand Jesus a little bit more. As I tell my students, if you aren't willing to ask questions, then how can you expect to find any answers? So, the fact that you've asked this question—Who is Jesus?—helped lead you to this book. Or, maybe you've met Him and know a little bit about Him already but you just want to know a little more about Jesus; that is still questioning, isn't it? So, let's get into this a little bit, shall we?

Jesus, the myth, the legend, the superstar, the real person.

Who is Jesus?

Believe it or not, the majority of people, especially Americans (an estimated ninety two percent, as of the research when writing this first draft in 2022), believe that Jesus was a real person. That's great news! But believing one is a real person does not automatically equate to one believing anything else said about that person, i.e. God's Son, savior, still alive. But we will get into some other aspects about Jesus, the real person, a little later in this book. However, there are still some people that do not hold to this belief; they claim Jesus never truly existed—that He is a fictional character created to tell the greatest story ever told.

The greatest story ever told by more than 40 different authors in three different languages (Hebrew,

Aramaic, and Greek) through 66 books and spanning over a 1,500 year period. All that is true. But like I mentioned earlier about asking questions, I've often wondered how more than 40 authors, speaking different languages, living in different cultures and time periods, in the days before the internet when the world was so big, separated, and communication was mostly limited to the local region, could write such a unified love story pointing to one person, one God, one hope. Not only that, but they detail the same patterns. Some people believe it is all just coincidence, a random happenstance, like the old theory "if an infinite number of monkeys were left to bang on an infinite number of typewriters, sooner or later they would accidentally reproduce the complete works of William Shakespeare." Sure, there's always a chance for everything, especially if everything was created by random; because that would then mean there is no order, no absolute, no universal anything, but that anything could happen at any given moment and given enough time, even if that time required would be a googolplex, which is a 1 followed by 100 zeros. By the logic of change over time (the definition of evolution), then any random thing, even the theory of monkey's hammering away on typewriters and producing the complete works of William Shakespeare would be possible and therefore should be accepted as a valid theory.

Where am I going with this?

Well, your foundation is one of two worldviews: God is real and created everything or everything was produced by random chance over an infinite amount of time. Meaning, whether you believe in God or not, we would all arrive at the same answer to this question: how could more than 40 authors, speaking different languages, living in different cultures and time periods, write such a unified love story pointing to one person, one God, one hope—because it's a true story and all the characters are real and true. Remember, you believe in God and all that his Word says or you don't believe in God but must admit that all that could very well be true, given enough time.

Anyway, some people also believe that Jesus was just a prophet, nothing special, but a prophet no different than one speaking what is considered universal wisdom like that of Confucius, Socrates, and many others throughout history. This belief states that Jesus had some wise words, speaking some wisdom about the universal concept of peace and acceptance of all through love, regardless. But even this concept does not capture the full and complete person that was and is Jesus, nor does it hold weight against the teachings of Jesus himself—yes, he loved people, but not everyone would be considered his sheep, his followers, God's children. Remember, Jesus said in John 14:6 that "No one comes to the Father except through me."

I want you to know that Jesus was and is a real person, and that Jesus is not just a person, but He is also divine in nature; Jesus is humanity's savior.

Did I just use a present tense and a past tense in one sentence to describe a person? Yes.

But how can that be? Someone either was or is or will be. That is correct. Jesus was a real person; He is a real person; and He will forever be a real person.

I will explain this a little later on.

Jesus was a real person; is a real person; and will forever be a real person.

But for now it is important to understand that history, archeology, and personal testimonies, all do point to the fact that Jesus was a real person. He really existed; He really walked on this earth.

But what else is there about Jesus? Is He more than just a person? Is there more to Him that I not only should know but that I need to know?

I do hope, and, since you are reading this, I do believe, that if you continue reading this whole book, the answers about Jesus will become clearer to you.

We all have a choice in this life, we can learn and grow and walk with Jesus or we can remain ignorant and shrink and push Jesus out of our lives. I am happy you have chosen to at least learn a little more about Jesus. I believe this choice will be a great experience for you in getting to know who Jesus is and to begin your journey to, hopefully, overflowing with Jesus.

We all have a choice in this life, we can learn and grow and walk with Jesus or we can remain ignorant and shrink and push Jesus out of our lives.

Chapter 2:

Introduction

"A leader is one who knows the way, goes the way, and shows the way."

John C. Maxwell[1]

Tim and Holly are a lovely young couple who have only been married for a few short years. Because of their financial situation and work schedules when they first tied the knot, they were forced to postpone what they viewed as a true honeymoon. They have lived a happy marriage life, and even though it took them a few years of saving and sacrificing, they were finally in a position to enjoy their true honeymoon.

They scheduled the flights, reserved the hotel, marked out their plan for shopping (her idea), sightseeing, and, of course, the normal honeymoon things.

Florida, here they come!

Their bags were packed, the house was closed, the cats were fed, the plants were watered, and they just turned the key, locking the door; and then the phone rang.

Ring. Ring. Ring.

Holly reached into her purse and fished around for a moment, moving her wallet, lipstick, sunglasses, and other various items lost in the vastness of space which is the inside of a woman's purse.

Ah, ha! The phone.

Holly pulled out her phone and answered the call. She looked at Tim and then walked a few feet away while she finished her conversation.

Holly hung up her phone and looked at Tim.

"Let me guess," said Tim, "that was work?"

"It's okay," answered Holly, "it's a quick business trip."

"But we are on vacation; we're taking our honeymoon," pleaded Tim.

"I'm sorry, but work calls," said Holly. She continued, "It's just one day. You can head to Florida ahead of me and get us all checked in. And then I can join you the next day. It's not a problem."

Being the good husband Tim is, he said, "Yes, dear."

Tim and Holly hugged, kissed, and then departed for their destinations.

When Tim arrived at the hotel in Florida, he checked them both in, and then he pulled out his phone and decided he would send Holly a quick email to update her. While typing the email, he had a brilliant idea—he would be super romantic by adding a sense of mystery to his message.

He quickly typed his romantic, mysterious, and informative message, and then typed in her email address. He reviewed his message, smiling while he reread it.

She will love this, he thought to himself.

He hit send—Whoosh—and the email was on its way. Unfortunately, Tim never doublechecked the address, which he mistyped in the "To:" section.

Anne made her way to her computer. Anne was a widow. Her and her husband had been married for fifty-four years. Her husband was a lifelong minister who had just passed away a few weeks prior.

Anne lived alone and thought that checking her email on her computer might help take her mind off of her grief from losing her husband. She opened her email—DING!—a new message arrived.

She clicked on the email and began to read it. After a few seconds, she screamed. Her scream was so loud that it penetrated through the walls of her home and entered the home of her neighbors. Then, Anne passed out and fell to the floor.

Anne's neighbors rushed over, banged on her door, and when there was no answer, they busted the door down. They ran through the house shouting, "Anne! Anne, are you okay!?"

They found Anne lying on the floor, a look of terror etched on her face, passed out completely.

They slowly approached and noticed her email open on her computer.

It read:

Dearest Wife,

I just got checked in and everything is prepared for your arrival tomorrow.

P.S.

It sure is hot down here.[2]

Relationships are Person-al

Through the next six chapters, we will look into who Jesus is and what the Bible says about Jesus; we will also look at what the Bible says about our relationship to and with Jesus. In other words, through the next few chapters (this book, really) we will explore a few aspects of Jesus—these are by no means the only ones, but they are important ones to know and understand.

A relationship with Jesus is all for your benefit.

I hope that by the end of this book you will have a greater concept of who Jesus is and that you will have grown deeper in your faith and deeper in your relationship with Him.

The following chapters will cover different aspects of Jesus and, hopefully, make it very clear as to how all these aspects fit together for your benefit. Yes, for your benefit; a relationship with Jesus is all for your benefit; it's about glory and honor to God, but you benefit fully from it. Once you learn more about who Jesus is, then you, too, will begin to see why I would claim these aspects fit together for your benefit.

The following is a list of what the coming chapters will contain.

JESUS THE PERSON

If Jesus is not a person, then how can we have a personal relationship with Him?

Relationships are Person-al (pun intended).

JESUS OUR SAVIOR

There is only one person who can truly save us. I'll give you a hint: it's not us and our good works.

JESUS OUR SANCTIFIER

Only one person can set us apart from the world and free us from sin.

JESUS OUR HEALER

Only one name is powerful enough to conquer hell and the grave, and to cleanse us.

JESUS OUR COMING KING & LIVING MISSIONALLY

Only one person, only one God, has ever truthfully claimed He will return to save His people. Only one person has ever risen from the grave and ascended to Heaven.

We are all called to be "fishers of men" (Matthew 4:19 NCSV). We are all to seek to reflect Jesus in our lives—to want to try and live more Christlike—and we are all to share Him with others—to preach His gospel to the ends of the earth.

If Jesus is not a person, then how can we have a personal relationship with Him?

Chapter 3:

Who is Jesus?

"If you have an important point to make, don't try to be subtle or clever. Use a pile driver. Hit the point once. Then come back and hit it again. Then hit it a third time - a tremendous whack."

Winston Churchill[1]

Throughout this book, we will be answering the question, "Who is Jesus?" But you already knew that, didn't you? That's why you are still reading this book. Well, Jesus is more than what can be contained in the few pages of this book; however, He can also be comprehended as easy as it would be to comprehend aspects of anyone so long as you are willing to open your arms and invite a stranger into your home and have an honest, candid conversation with them.

So, the first step is to choose to seek—truly choose to seek—and then you shall find. But you must be willing to first want to find the Truth and then ask the question, "Who is Jesus?"

Who is Jesus?

This is such an important question to ask and to seek the Truth on; and, yet, even when we find an answer to this question, we still have one more question to answer—it is a deeper, more personal, and, for some, a difficult question to truthfully answer. Most often we already know this answer deep down inside us but we are frightful of accepting it or even openly admitting it.

In Matthew 16:13, Jesus is talking to His disciples and He asks them, "Who do people say the Son of Man is?" In other words, Jesus is asking them who people (the world) says He is?

To better understand this question, you must know a little bit about the time frame, culture, and society of that time. The gist of it, according to my knowledge and breakdown, is this: During the time that Jesus was alive and asking this question, the Jewish people had already been hearing much talk (gossip and news spread around the land) about someone who heals and speaks with wisdom and authority. This intrigued some and infuriated many others. Why? Because it was believed by the Jewish religion of that time that only God heals miraculously; only the Pharisees speak with wisdom because of their years of study in the Torah and their education of the law—the Old Testament; and only the Pharisees speak with authority from their work in the temple. The people did not have, and could not yet have, that personal relationship with God because Jesus had yet to fulfill his mission on this Earth.

So, obviously, this news of someone, a person, healing the sick, the blind, the lame, performing miracles, not trained like the Pharisees were and someone who did not hold a seat in the Sanhedrin, speaking with great wisdom and authority, was the talk of the town. This news spread like wildfire. The Sanhedrin was considered the supreme court of ancient Israel where all the questions pertaining to the law (Jewish law and God's law) were brought. Their word was usually final.

It might have even been considered an attack on the position, power, and authority of the Pharisees and the law itself by many of the people. Based on their belief and the understanding passed down from those in charge, a person who healed, spoke with great wisdom, and who walked with such authority could only be sent from God... or be God himself. However, even though their very belief formed by the prophets of old, whom they cherished and trusted, and God's very Word, told them about Jesus (not by specific name), they still considered it heresy and blasphemy to believe that Jesus was the Son of God. They believed he was merely another prophet, albeit one that was a challenge to the positions of power and authority held by those in the Sanhedrin.

> *The world will always have an opinion, and its opinion will always be in favor of its own justification.*

The Sanhedrin was not a political party like we might think of in modern times, nor was it just a corrupted form of government. On the contrary, this system was established by God Himself for the Jewish people of the Old Testament. In Numbers 11:16 God commanded Moses to "Bring me seventy of Israel's elders who are known to you as leaders and officials among the people. Have them come to the tent of meeting, that they may stand there with you. I will come down and speak with you there, and I will take some of the power of the Spirit that is on you and put it on them. They will share the burden of the people with you so that you will not have to carry it alone."

Throughout the generations, the Jewish people had been waiting for the arrival of the Messiah, the one who would free them from their bondage, free them from their Roman oppressors, and bring judgment upon the enemies of God. There had already been one man, named John the Baptist, who had been boldly proclaiming the coming of "the one who comes after me, the straps of whose sandals I am not worthy to untie" (John 1:27). John had been standing firm in his faith in God and the words of the prophets and the teachings of God's law to the people, which was the Torah: the first five books of the Hebrew Bible (the first five books of the Holy Bible: Genesis, Exodus, Leviticus, Numbers and Deuteronomy). John was even so bold as to call out the leaders of his day for their sins against God, for their unbelief, for their false teachings… even to their faces at times. Someone this bold in that time period and in that culture must have either been insane mentally or empowered by God.

So, rumors were spreading, hope was brewing, oppression was strong, confidence was building, expectations were high, and people were confused.

Sounds familiar, doesn't it?

Well, when Jesus asked them, "Who do people say the Son of Man is?" the disciples replied, "Some say John the Baptist; others say Elijah (a prophet of the Old Testament); and still others, Jeremiah or one of the prophets." Well, if Jesus was Elijah, then he truly would just be a man and nothing more than that. If Jesus was Jeremiah or one of the prophets from the past, then the same would be true—just a man— because they were great prophets and men of faith, but they were not sinless and they most certainly were not the Son of God. So they at least had a tiny bit of an answer—Jesus was a man, but He was also so much more than that.

Everyone had their opinions, deductions, and conclusions about who the Son of Man was—Elijah, Jeremiah, and other prophets who were already dead and gone—and who the Son of Man is—John the Baptist was alive and well, causing havoc for the wicked people and rulers by proclaiming God's Word and law and boldly calling out their sins, even publicly if needed, all in the name of love, to save the people, to get them to repent.

Truth without love can be harsh, but love without truth is deception.

The world will always have an opinion, and its opinion will always be in favor of its own justification.

It is easier to twist and justify morality and truth in order to continue to live a chosen lifestyle and in one's own way then it is to change one's lifestyle and way to fit morality and Truth.

Love without truth is deception.

Jesus wasn't really interested in what the world said, for He knew the world. The "world" is also those who do not believe in Jesus, those who do not follow God, and those who choose the kingdom of this world, and the ruler of the kingdom of this world is Satan.

"You adulterous people!" Jesus was calling people out for their doublethink—holding two contradictory ideas, or beliefs, simultaneously and believing that both of them are true—the world, especially the Pharisees at that time, claimed to believe in God, but at the same time they also believed the world. They were playing both sides for their own benefit. Then He went on to say, "Don't you know that friendship with the world [Satan] means enmity with God? Therefore, anyone who chooses to be a friend of the world becomes an enemy of God" (James 4:4). You cannot serve two masters. There are no double agents here. You believe in Jesus and follow God, or you disbelieve Jesus and follow the world.

Jesus said in John 17:14-16, "I have given them your word [God's Word] and the world has hated them, for they are not of the world any more than I am of the world. My prayer is not that you take them out of the world but that you protect them from the evil one [Satan]. They are not of the world, even as I am not of it."

Jesus knew that this world is a fallen world, He knew that when we accept Him and are born again that we are no longer of this world any longer either. This world will always rebuke, mock, and push Jesus away, that is why He was not truly interested in what the world thought of Him or who the world thought was and is the Son of Man. Jesus wanted to hear what the disciples thought, in their own words just as He wants to know what you think, in your own words.

Jesus asked Simon Peter, "But what about you? Who do you say I am?"

Jesus wants to know what you truly believe; He wants to know who you say He is.

"Simon Peter answered, 'You are the Messiah, the Son of the living God.'"

Jesus wants to know what you truly believe: who do you say He is?

My hope is that this book will help answer that question everyone asks in their life: "Who is Jesus?" And I hope that after reading this book, you will be better able to personally answer the other question: Who do you say Jesus is?

I hope everyone reading this book will be better equipped to answer those two questions in their life:

- Who is Jesus?

- Who do you say Jesus is?

I also hope that, after reading this book, you will choose to overflow with Jesus in all aspects of your life.

No matter our education or spiritual level, there is always more to learn in, about, and from God, the Bible, and Jesus.

And although we are called to preach the good news, it is best if we, as believers (when you accept Jesus into your heart as your Lord and Savior, then you are a believer), do not neglect our gathering together and encouraging each other and learning more.

We want to grow in our understanding so that we can communicate the Gospel to everyone as clearly as we can and not be so mysterious that we scare little old ladies, like Tim did in the story in Chapter 2.

Chapter 4:

Jesus the Person

"As to Jesus of Nazareth…I think the system of morals and his religion, as he left them to us, the best the world ever saw or is likely to see."

Benjamin Franklin[1]

Jane was the mayor of her town, and having been the mayor for ten years, she certainly had made her connections. If she had a strong foundation, then maybe her career path would not have been marked with so many potholes—if you know what I mean.

Anyway, after so many years of serving in politics, she became used to being able to do a lot of what she wanted and getting away with it, too. In fact, her life quotes had become, "life is short, do what you want," and, "do as I say, not as I do." Her morality was weak, shaky, and in constant flux; her morality became what she wanted.

One day, Jane was speeding down the road in her Corvette Convertible, weaving in and out of traffic, rolling through stop signs, and running red lights.

This type of behavior behind the wheel was not unusual for her; if she got pulled over, she just dropped some prominent and powerful names, names that carried authority, and then she was let off with only a warning. It never failed.

However, this day was different.

Jane flew through the red light—ZOOM!!!

A few seconds later she noticed flashing red and blue lights reflecting in her rear-view mirror.

Jane sighed in disgust, and then angrily whispered to herself, "You are wasting my time."

She pulled over and impatiently waited for the

inevitable speech: This is just a warning. I'm sorry to have bothered you, Ma'am. Have a nice day.

As she waited and rehearsed her lines in her head, the Officer walked up to her and gave his normal speech: "License and registration, please."

Jane, rudely, answered back with the names of people she knew in high positions.

The Officer waited for her to finish and then replied with the same command, "License and registration, please."

She threw her license at the Officer and then, impatiently, she said, "Do you know who I am?"

The Officer picked up her license, looked at it, and then said, "Yes. According to your license, your name is Jane. And you were caught violating the law."

Jane snapped back, "You don't know who you are talking too!"

The Officer interrupted her and said, "It also says here that you wear glasses. I don't see you wearing your glasses."

Jane screamed, "I have contacts!"

To which the Officer replied, "I don't care who your contacts are, you are still guilty."[2]

Our contact holds ultimate authority.

Historically, Jesus has been shown to be a real person. Archeologists have dug up evidence pointing to many different biblical figures and events, each pointing to the time as indicated in the biblical texts. There is little debate now that even science has backed up the claim that Jesus did exist.

So, obviously, in this chapter we will discuss and learn about THE PERSON OF JESUS.

There might be some things I speak of here that might not make complete sense to you when you read them, but if you bear with me, in time, they will begin to make sense.

Jesus was born in Bethlehem a little over 2,000 years ago (from the writing of this book). He was born of a virgin named Mary. Mary was impregnated by God—God did not sleep with her as some people might incorrectly believe or even outright mock. It clearly states in Scripture that "Before I [God] formed you in the womb I knew you" (Jeremiah 1:5). God forms us in our mother's womb. Yes, there is a scientific process that occurs when a man and a woman come together, but it is God who creates life, not man. Therefore, God created life in Mary, and that life was Jesus.

Jesus was born human, and He became a grown man; therefore, Jesus was a man. Makes sense, right? But He was also the Son of God and God; He is part of the Trinity. I know this part can sound ridiculous at first and hard to comprehend, but if you truly desire to know and understand, then it will be made clearer to you as you read on.

Anyway, Jesus, through Him becoming man (that

is, God becoming human), and living a sinless life on this earth, and dying for our sins and our eternal salvation—He became our contact with God.

1 Peter 2:22 says, "He [Jesus] committed no sin, and no deceit was found in his mouth."

Jesus was the only person to live upon this earth who did not commit sin, who was not found guilty of deceit or wickedness or wrongdoing. He was the only person to be fully righteous.

Prior to this time, God did not dwell in humans; in fact, God typically only spoke with humans through one person—a prophet. This prophet would be the only person God would speak to, and this person would communicate what God said to the people. Believe it or not, there was a period of about four hundred years where God did not speak to one person on this earth. Wickedness reigned, and the people did what was right in their own eyes. They lived without a firm and absolute foundation; thus, their morality was whatever they wanted. And when one has no firm foundation, no absolute morality for their life, they can very easily justify every action against their neighbor and God. With no firm foundation, one becomes that which they hate; then they love that which they become because what they become is always moral and right in their own sight.

During the time before Jesus, there was a period when God dwelt with his people in a tent called the Holy of Holies.

But because of our contact, Jesus Christ, bridging that gap between God and man, God now dwells in each of us who accept Him and believe in His son Jesus as our Lord and Savior.

Because God loved us so much, He came down to earth, became human, and He died for us.

John 3:16 says, "For God so loved the world that he gave his one and only Son, that whoever believes in him shall not perish but have eternal life."

Aren't you glad we, too, have a contact? But unlike Jane in our story opening this chapter, our contact is Jesus, who can and did save us from our sins and brought redemption through Grace, not our inability to follow every command of the law. Our contact in Jesus washes our sins away, and we are found not guilty. Our contact holds ultimate authority.

Jesus became our contact with God.

When you allow the Person of Jesus to be your friend, and when you accept him into your heart to be your savior, then you have accepted God's grace through faith, and all this is made possible through our friend, the Person of Jesus. As it says in Romans 6:14, "For sin shall no longer be your master, because you are not under the law, but under grace."

Yeah, I have a contact. He is the Son of the King, and he pardoned my sin, my inability to keep from violating the law, and that goes for you, too, if you choose. "For we maintain that a person is justified by faith apart from the works of the law" (Romans 3:28).

He, too, can be your contact with the one true

God.

Believe it or not, all religions, even atheists, cannot deny that the Person of Jesus truly existed; that Jesus was a real person. There is no doubt, through historical and archeological evidence, that Jesus was a real person.

So, what does the world do? They deny another aspect of Jesus, the most important aspect of Him. They question His divinity. When they deny His divinity, they deny Christ Himself. They claim He was not the Son of God, not God, that He did not die for our sins, and that He did not rise again, and they deny God's very own words when Jesus said, "I am the way and the truth and the life. No one comes to the Father except through me" (John 14:6).

But, since we are talking about the Person of Jesus in this chapter, I want to ask you, "What does the person of Jesus mean to you today?"

People die, flesh rots, and bones decay; eventually nothing of our physical body remains on this earth— unless you are mummified or fossilized, but even that won't last forever. But the soul will last forever.

I do find it interesting, though, that some people, even some who claim to be believers in God, might still have a problem believing that Jesus IS STILL a person.

When we die, our spirit goes to either Heaven or Hell, depending on whether we chose to accept and believe in Jesus or reject Him with our unbelief. God is not a cruel God, for He gives us what we want, what we choose: to be with Him or to remain apart from Him.

And if, when we die, our spirit is either in Heaven or Hell, where did Jesus go?

Jesus bore our sins upon the cross (we will get into this more in a later chapter), and because He took our sins upon Himself, He went to Hell (He took our place in our judgment); but He was only there for three days, just long enough to suffer our judgment so we could be saved and to take the power and authority away from Satan. Then He rose again.

So, if Jesus died and rose, then He is in Heaven, right? Yes, because He rose again and ascended to Heaven.

Jesus is one-third of the Trinity: the Father, the Son, the Holy Spirit (also referred to as the Holy Ghost, but I prefer the term Spirit).

But Jesus is God; God is Jesus.

Not just that, but after Jesus rose again, He presented Himself, nail holes in His hands and feet and scars and wounds and all, to His disciples and many others as recorded in writing. It is human beings, people, a person who has a human body, and it is the human body that shows scars and wounds.

But as I was saying, we have: God the Father, God the Son, God the Holy Spirit.

They are all God. Three in one. The Trinity.

The Holy Spirit is God, Jesus is God, and it states

in John 16:13-15, about the Holy Spirit, "But when **he**, the Spirit of truth, comes, **he** will guide you into all the truth. **He** will not speak on **his** own; **he** will speak only what **he** hears, and **he** will tell you what is yet to come. **He** will glorify me because it is from me that **he** will receive what **he** will make known to you. All that belongs to the Father is mine. That is why I said the Spirit will receive from me what **he** will make known to you."

The Bible even calls the Holy Spirit a person: He.

To live with the Holy Spirit is to live with Jesus.

And Jesus said, "All that belongs to the Father is mine." Because He is God, God is Jesus.

God is spiritual, yes; but God is also a person—the Person of Jesus.

Through the Person of Jesus, God walked the earth, He talked on this earth, He experienced all the emotions that we experience on this earth, He made friendships, He built relationships with people, He made that personal connection with Him possible through Him.

And He dwells in us and guides us and speaks to us through the Holy Spirit.

Through Jesus, through the Person of Jesus, experiencing this life and sacrificing His life, He made that personal connection with God possible.

Through the Person of Jesus, we can now have that personal relationship with God.

To live with the Holy Spirit is to live with Jesus.

John 16:23-24 says, "In that day you will no longer ask me anything. Very truly I tell you, my Father will give you whatever you ask **in my name**. Until now you have not asked for anything in my name. Ask and you will receive, and your joy will be complete."

Two verses later Jesus says, "In that day you will ask **in my name**. I am not saying that I will ask the Father on your behalf" (John 16:26-28).

Why? Why would Jesus, our friend, tell us that He would not ask the Father (God) on our behalf? I thought Jesus was our contact with God? He is our contact, but through His sacrifice, He made it possible for us to accept God's grace and have the Holy Spirit (God) live in us; that is how we become the temple. As it states in 1 Corinthians 3:16-17, "Don't you know that you yourselves are God's temple and that God's Spirit dwells in your midst? If anyone destroys God's temple, God will destroy that person; for God's temple is sacred, and you together are that temple."

Because when we believe in Jesus, we begin to establish that personal relationship with God through the Holy Spirit and have that power and speak with authority in the name of Jesus.

A personal relationship is a relationship between persons; therefore, you cannot have a personal relationship unless He is a person.

It continues, in John, to say, "No, the Father himself loves you because you have loved me and have believed that I came from God. I came from the Father and entered the world; now I am leaving the world and going back to the Father" (John 16:27-28).

Love. God loves you. Jesus loves you. God is love. Love is kind, not nice. As I say in another book titled *Truth: A Courageous Journey to Discover the Truth That Will Never Fail You*, "Both [kindness and niceness] mean that you treat other people well, but only one speaks the truth... To be nice means that you can lie; it is sometimes motivated by a selfish desire to appear to be good, or, in some cases, to avoid conflict... Kindness shows a deeper level of care, a deeper level of empathy, a deeper level of love. Sometimes to be kind, you must show love in the way of teaching, rebuking, correcting, and training in the truth, and this will rarely come without some conflict." Kindness will not always be seen as nice, because niceness will not always speak in love, but kindness is to love, for love without truth is deception.

The world likes to mock and warp what God says, and in doing so they like to repeat the phrase "Love is Love." It sounds great, but it is not biblical. God is love, but love is not God. Exodus 20:3 says, "You shall have no other gods before me." If love is God, then love is the god. For God created all things (Colossians 1:16), He even created love; but love did not create God, therefore, God is love, but love is not God. There is no other above God. Love should not become your idol. God is love, and God disciplines and corrects.

Love corrects, it prunes, it disciplines; love does

not accept evil, wickedness, or lies. "Your eyes are too pure to look on evil; you cannot tolerate wrongdoing" (Habakkuk 1:13).

Proverbs 3:11-12 says, "My son, do not despise the LORD's discipline, and do not resent his rebuke, because the LORD disciplines those he loves, as a father the son he delights in."

Love is a choice. Just as creating and having a relationship with someone is a choice.

Orson Welles didn't know how close he was to being correct when he said, "We're born alone, we live alone, we die alone. Only through our **love** and **friendship** can we create the illusion for the moment that we're not alone."[3]

When we are born, our spirit is dead; we are alone apart from God.

Proverbs 18:1 (NKJV) says, "A man who isolates himself seeks his own desires; he rages against all wise judgment..."

Without a relationship with our friend and Savior the Person of Jesus, we are truly alone. We may, as Orson Wells said, "create the illusion for the moment that we're not alone," but spiritually, we are alone.

Without Jesus, we live alone and we die alone; we are barren—we live and die apart from God. It is through our love for Jesus and our relationship with God through the Person of Jesus that we truly have life and life more abundantly.

Ann Landers—who was an American advice

columnist—said, "Love is friendship that has caught fire. It is quiet understanding, mutual confidence, sharing and forgiving. It is loyalty through good and bad times. It settles for less than perfection and makes allowances for human weaknesses."[4]

If only she knew how true this is when you come into a personal relationship with Jesus.

Love is a choice. Friendship is created through relationship. When you choose to love Jesus, you begin to build that relationship and create that personal friendship with God, then that personal relationship catches fire through the Holy Spirit.

Friendship and Relationship require people—You and the Person of Jesus.

Jesus is that quiet understanding, which is peace; He is the Prince of Peace (Isaiah 9:6).

Jesus is that mutual confidence when we desire to live like Him.

Jesus is our friend in whom we can share our most held secrets with, and He is our forgiveness.

Jesus is our friend in whom we can trust in the good and bad times; He will never leave nor forsake you (Deuteronomy 31:8).

Jesus is our perfection, our righteousness, our Savior, our Sanctifier, our Healer, our King, our friend.

It is through our friend, through our personal relationship with the Person of Jesus that our failings and sins are forgiven; through the Person of Jesus,

God made allowances for our human weaknesses by His sacrifice on the cross for us all. God's saving grace is evident through Jesus.

It is through the Person of Jesus that we are also shown how to live our lives.

Jesus' personality drew people, His character was pure and just and sinless.

1 John 2:6 says, "Whoever claims to live in him must live as Jesus did."

We must strive to live as the Person of Jesus.

It is through God's Word that He guides us how to live, and it was through the Person of Jesus that God showed us how to live.

His character was: Compassionate, Servant, Focused and obedient to God's will, Forgiving, Loving (but not without correction when one does evil), Honesty (he was a man of his word, because He is the Word), Intimate (with those who chose to follow him and with God the Father through prayer), and He walked with authority in God's Word.

To be Christ-like is not to tolerate sin, but to walk in truth and love as Jesus did.

To be Christ like is to invite Jesus into your heart, to have that personal relationship with Him, and to seek to walk in His ways. It is not to accept, affirm, condone, or tolerate every lifestyle choice, because that is not love and that is not Christ-like.

The idea that Jesus tolerated all beliefs, religions,

or lifestyles is not truth. The Person of Jesus did not walk the earth validating choices that violated God's Word. Instead, He consistently rebuked sin, hypocrisy, unbelief, and corruption—all from God's standards.

He did not once tolerate evil or wickedness.

Jesus rebuked hypocrisy and false teaching as evident in Matthew 23:13-36 when he called the Pharisees "hypocrites," "blind guides," "blind fools," "whitewashed tombs," "brood of vipers."

Jesus rebuked them for shutting "the door of the kingdom of heaven in people's faces", for false teachings, for their inward corruption and disguise of outward righteousness, and for leading people astray. Their religion was an external one—pride and power—not internal—love and obedience. They rejected the Truth and therefore rejected Jesus.

He drove out the money changers from the temple in John 2:13-16 and Matthew 21. Greed took over and they used God's house to exploit the people, dishonesty was the game, and thievery was their name.

He spoke of warnings for those who would lead people astray. Astray from what? God's standards. In Mathew 18:6-7 he said, "If anyone causes one of these little ones ... to stumble, it would be better for them to have a large millstone hung around their neck and to be drowned in the depths of the sea." He continues this warning through verse 7. Jesus warns of the peril for causing little ones to stumble. Who are these "little one's"? Just before this, in Matthew 18:3, Jesus said, "Truly I tell you, unless you change and become like little children, you will never enter the kingdom of heaven." The "little one's" refers to believers, those who believe in Jesus Christ as Lord and Savior, as the Son of God, who died for their sins and rose again. Romans 14:13 warns of causing a believer's faith to be corrupted, as those who cause others to stumble and fall spiritually, God holds them accountable.

In Revelation 2-3, Jesus rebuked the churches for tolerating sin—false teachings, immorality, and idolatry. But how could this be if to be Christ-like is to accept, affirm, condone, validate, and even participate with all beliefs, lifestyles, and choices? Jesus showed zero tolerance for what God calls sin, instead speaking of repentance (turning away from sin) and holiness (being set apart with God).

In Mathew and John, we read of Jesus walking away from unbelief. Once those made their choice in their heart, set as hard as stone, He walked away; Jesus did not compromise His values or the Truth (the Word of God).

Jesus was always consistent in His rebuke of sin, unbelief, hypocrisy, and false teachings. He did not once tolerate evil or wickedness. He walked away from people who chose to reject Him, giving them what they wanted—to be separated from God and all that God is. Jesus clearly showed us that God's Truth stands above all; that God's Truth—the Word of God—His standards, would not be and could not be compromised by the worldly standards or human thinking.

So, to be Christ-like is to follow Jesus. It is to not accept, affirm, condone, validate, participate, or even tolerate sin, but to walk in both Truth and love. To be Christ-like is to show true love, which can only come from God, and this love is to call people to repentance and holiness. To be Christ-like is to believe in Jesus, embrace him as friend, Savior, Lord, to obey God's Word, to set your standards and values to God's standards and values, to reject the world's false and corrupted idea that love means to accept, affirm, condone, validate, participate, or even tolerate what God calls sin, wicked.

It is by our decision to read God's Word so we might fill our thoughts with God and grow and live, as best as we can, Christ-like lives, that we truly show our love for God and our true friendship with the Person of Jesus.

"In our thoughts we create our destiny, with our words we inspire our destiny, through our actions we move toward our destiny, because of our repeated habits we form our destiny, and based on the character we have allowed ourselves to become we shape and live our destiny."[5]

Jesus, our friend with whom we have that personal relationship with, wants us to have a destiny full of life.

It is the Person of Jesus, His character, which we should strive to emulate.

Chapter 5:

Jesus our Savior

*"How sweet it is to learn the Savior's love when nobody else loves us!
When friends flee, what a blessed thing it is to see that the Savior
does not forsake us but still keeps us and holds us fast and clings to us
and will not let us go!"*

Charles Spurgeon[1]

There were two brothers: Nathan, who was barely a teenager, and Josiah, who was only eight years old. Josiah, being the younger brother, tended to look up to and follow his older brother Nathan. This was a problem for their parents.

Nathan, being a teenager now, devolved the thought pattern that seems to be inherent in children when they reach that age demographic. Nathan did not like rules nor did he like being told what to do by anyone, including his parents; and since Josiah followed his older brother, he, too, at the age of eight, began to act in a similar manner—although he was too young to fully comprehend why his older brother thought this way.

Nathan believed that he did not need rules or help from anyone because, at his newfound age of enlightenment, he knew all there was to know, and he believed he could save himself, and his younger brother, from any problem or situation, which they both often boasted about.

These two became troubled kids; they were very mischievous, and they were always causing trouble and getting into trouble.

Finally, their parents, after what felt like years of trying to correct, teach, protect, and hopefully save their boys from the path of destruction they were on (unbeknownst to the boys, but evident to their parents, especially their Father who had been a young, rambunctious boy himself), were finally reaching their breaking point. They could not take it much longer.

They could not handle the boy's mischief and boasting and arrogance any longer.

That is when the "ah, ha" moment presented itself to their Mother.

Their Mother was informed that there was a special guest speaker who was scheduled to speak at their church for an evening event. She was also informed that this speaker was a preacher himself and that he had a successful record as a youth pastor, where he would not only teach the children, but he was also effective at disciplining and reaching the young children and helping them correct their paths.

Their Mother was so excited to hear this news!

She immediately ran to her husband and told him all that she had heard about this speaker. She convinced her husband to take that evening off from work so the whole family could attend this church event.

The husband, being the good husband that he was, said, "Yes, dear."

The Mother exclaimed, "This will be wonderful!"

Neither one of them knew what to do any longer with their boys, and they had been close to losing their tempers with them, again.

That evening came and the whole family attended the event. Afterward, the Mother led her family to the front to talk with the Speaker. She explained their situation and asked him if he could help.

The Speaker said, "Absolutely."

The Speaker talked with the Pastor of the church and secured a room where he could talk with each boy privately.

The first one he spoke with was Josiah (the youngest).

He sat Josiah down in a chair and then he immediately turned to him and politely asked, "Where is God?"

Josiah did not answer; He just tensed up in the chair, frozen.

The Speaker asked Josiah again, but this time his voice was sterner, "Where is God?"

Josiah did not move a muscle. He didn't even blink.

The Speaker thought, *This is unusual. By now they have given me a generic answer to this question.*

So, the Speaker asked him again, this time he was louder and even more intense with his question, "Where is God?"

Josiah still did not move; he did not say a word; he just sat there, a look of fear and worry upon his face, and sweat began to appear on his forehead. But still no answer.

The Speaker thought, *I don't get it. Maybe if I try to be more direct he will finally give me an answer.*

The Speaker leaned in close to Josiah, pointed his finger directly at the young boy, and, in a lower but more intense and authoritative tone, he asked, "Where is God?"

This time, he got a response from Josiah; but it was not the response he was hoping for or expecting.

Josiah immediately jumped up from his chair and bolted out of the room. He ran past his family, out of the church and directly home, where he locked himself in his closet.

His parents were confused and frightened for their child. They ran after him but, because of their confused hesitation, they lost him.

The first place they went to check was their home. Josiah's Mother, Father, and older brother, Nathan, all ran in the house shouting his name. They split up and began to search for him.

Nathan found Josiah hiding in his closet. When he saw him, he immediately embraced his little brother and then asked him, "Mom and dad are worried. Are you okay?"

Josiah, visibly shaken and scared, replied, "We are in big trouble. How can we be saved this time?"

Nathan was confused. He asked, "What happened?"

Josiah said, "God is missing. And they think we did it!"[2]

Whew! Aren't you glad God does not need us to save Him? If He did, all of us would be in for a very rude awakening; I mean, we cannot even save ourselves.

Aren't you glad God will never go missing? He will

never leave nor forsake us.

Aren't you glad God doesn't need us to save Him? And aren't you glad God will never go missing; He will never leave nor forsake us. Hebrews 13:5 says, "I will never leave you nor forsake you." I felt this needed to be repeated.

We can, however, leave and forsake God and become lost to ourselves, but we are never left, forsaken, or lost to God; it will break His heart if we reject Him, for He loves each of us, but He will honor our decision. Remember, God so loved the world that He sent His one and only Son to bear our sins for us so that we might be saved.

So, Jesus our Savior.

Merriam-Webster defines savior as "one who saves from danger or destruction," and "one who brings salvation."[3]

And salvation is "deliverance from sin and its consequences."[4]

Has anyone ever brought you salvation? Freed you from the curse of sin? Saved you from the judgment and punishment of your sin? Only one person ever has, and only one person ever could: the Person of Jesus.

From the beginning of the end, humanity has lived in desperate need of a savior.

[The beginning of the end is what I like to call the time of Genesis, where God speaks of Adam and Eve—the first people; the two who ate of the tree of the knowledge of good and evil, then hid from God, lied to God, accused each other and God, and then were kicked out of the Garden of Eden because of their willful decision to sin and not repent, and began our separation from God through sin.]

We were all, and many still are, in need of a savior.

I wish I could take credit for this insight, but I must give credit to the person whom credit is due (at least from whom I heard it from).

Ken Ham, author of many books, such as *The New Answers Book*, and a Christian Fundamentalist, had a documentary video series where he spoke on Dinosaurs and the Bible[5]. In that video, he mentioned, and I'm paraphrasing here, that in order to believe in evolution or the millions of years theory, then you would have to disbelieve in the Bible.

You cannot simultaneously hold to, believe in, and live your life by, two opposing ideas: "No one can serve two masters. Either you will hate the one and love the other, or you will be devoted to the one and despise the other" (Matthew 6:24). This is termed "doublethink." And if you believe in Jesus, then you believe God's Word (that is, the Holy Bible) to be true—it is The Truth: "All Scripture is God-breathed and is useful for teaching, rebuking, correcting and training in righteousness" (2 Timothy 3:16).

You cannot serve two masters; you cannot serve two kings.

One says all life, everything ever created, all that is in this world and the unknown universe, was created from nothing—it was once believed to be a dead star but is now believed to be such a miniscule point of infinite density, with no explanation as to how it became, exploded and somehow created everything. That everything is chaos and random. And if it was all created by random, then have you wondered how there could be absolute scientific laws that never change and have always been; and these laws are required for life to even exist?

Anyway, it says that all life was created by random happenstance: from nothing, by nothing, for nothing, to end in nothing. That is kind of sad and depressing, isn't it? Life has no purpose except to live for the moment, to do whatever is moral and acceptable in your eyes at any given moment, because we are not here, we were not created, we do not exist for any purpose—without purpose, value is little; we are an accident, a roll of the dice, and soon we will not be; our life does not and will not matter.

The other says that life was created by a living God who loves us and wants to spend eternity with us. All that ever exists, everything ever created, all that is in this world and the unknown universe, was created by a loving, living God. That everything has an order and, as we would classify it, a scientific approach. That all life exists for a reason; we have a purpose: From God, by God, for God, to be with God. That is Truth; that is hope. Life has a purpose. There is an absolute morality. Not everything is good or moral or acceptable, and this firm and absolute foundation does not change for anyone or at any moment. We are not an accident. Our life does matter.

You cannot serve two masters; you cannot serve two kings.

Think about this: "why would anyone sacrifice their life if life held no value in and of itself? Life is important, and every life has worth."[6] You are loved, you are worthy in God's eyes, you are saved by the grace and mercy and love of God through His son Jesus, if you believe and if you so choose. Remember, just like Adam and Eve, and just like every person ever created, you have the free will to choose for yourself if you will accept, believe and embrace the love of God, your identity of worth and value in God, and choose to be saved.

Anyway, in that video, he has a great saying, and again, I'm paraphrasing here, "You don't fit God's Word into science; you fit science into God's Word." In other words, you start with the Bible as your foundation, and from that foundation things begin to make sense, and then you can find the answers. Once you do this, you start to notice something that is often overlooked or ignored—many of the dating methods used in science are dependent upon layers of assumptions. The preconceived conclusion isn't reached from the data; it's often reached by the requirement of the theory. In this case, the assumptions are modeled, shaped, and adjusted to lead one to the predetermined answer, and then that answer, that preconceived conclusion, is used to support, justify, and validate the assumptions.

Science, history, archeology, have all been proving the Bible accurate. It is awesome, and it is astonishing.

It is as God intended.

Anyway, the Bible clearly states that death entered through sin, and that sin entered this world through man sinning against God—when Adam and Eve chose to disobey God's command and chose, what we now might call, the world's understanding over God's understanding; they chose to eat of the tree of the knowledge of good and evil in order to know what God knows, because they did not trust God, and wanted to be like God instead of being one in God. When they chose unbelief rather than belief in God, that is when their spirit died.

The search for knowledge is not evil nor is it wrong; "As the saying goes, 'scientia potentia est,' or as we know it, 'knowledge is power.' Knowledge is power, but without wisdom, this power can be destructive and corrupt. Wisdom is the correct application of knowledge."[7] Adam and Eve, through the deception of Satan, desired knowledge, but without the foundation of God in their lives (the leading of the Holy Spirit which, by God's grace, He imparted into us through Jesus Christ), their acquired knowledge came without wisdom—the wisdom of God; his firm foundation. Thus their knowledge led them to understand the emotions and feelings of shame, regret, fear, and insecurity, and, in this newfound knowledge, they hid from God, blamed each other, blamed God, and showed a new birth in a corrupt nature and destroyed their spirit. It was only through God's grace and mercy and love that we could be forgiven and saved.

Granted, it was the devil (the father of lies—John 8:44) who whispered words of treachery and disbelief into the ears of Adam and Eve, influencing them to hand their authority over the land to him through their trust in him and unbelief in God. But God gives us all a choice, He gave us all free will. God loves each one of us; but love is not force or slavery. Love is a choice, and without Him giving us a choice to choose to love Him, we would not be free, nor could we claim "We love because he first loved us" (1 John 4:19).

Because Adam and Eve sinned, humanity was cursed with the punishment of death through sin.

Romans 5:12 says, "Therefore, just as sin entered the world through one man, and death through sin, and in this way death came to all people, because all sinned…"

We are all sinners—our Spirits are dead in Christ, until we choose Jesus as our Lord and Savior, then we are born again: Jesus is our Savior.

Until we can conquer sin, we will forever be unable to conquer death; and until we conquer death, sin will rule.

We were doomed by our own doing. We had one command, one rule, and we chose to be disobedient, we chose to not trust, we chose unbelief, and that was the beginning of the end for this world. No amount of good deeds or works on our part could ever atone for our sins.

It is by the grace of God, through faith in Jesus Christ, that we can be saved.

If you are confused about atonement, let me try to help: Atonement means "reparation," or "reconciliation."[8]

The Hebrew word for atonement is "Kippur" (kip-poor), which means "the covering or removal of a transgression."[9] Atonement is the covering of our sins by the blood of Jesus and our pardon from the judgment and curse of sin by the only person who could ever take our place—our friend, the Person of Jesus.

Transgression is a violation of a law; in this case, a violation against the law of God, or the moral law of God.

There was a time where all of humanity lived without law, they lived by their own morality, they did whatever they wanted, "everyone did as they saw fit" (Judges 17:6). Man could not figure out how to live a just, moral, righteous life, therefore, all were just and moral in their own sight, and all became self-righteous. Man could not figure out what was good, what was Godly, how to be their own savior—a futile endeavor, "for all have sinned and fall short of the glory of God" (Romans 3:23).

Then God gave the Israelites the Ten Commandments.

1. No other god before Him.

2. Do not make idols for your life

3. Do not take the name of the Lord your God in vain

4.   Keep the Sabbath day holy

5.   Honor your father and mother

6.   Do not murder

7.   Do not commit adultery

8.   Do not steal

9.   Do not lie

10.   Do not covet

Man needed instructions on how to live, because as we mentioned, "all have sinned and fall short of the glory of God."

We are all sinners, every single person; we are all sinners and we have all fallen short of the glory of God. And no amount of good works can ever outweigh our sins, no amount of good behavior or works can ever atone for our sins.

Ephesians 2:8-9 says, "For it is by grace you have been saved, through faith—and this is not from yourselves, it is the gift of God—not by works, so that no one can boast."

It is by the grace of God, through faith in Jesus Christ, that we can be saved.

Paul said in his letter to the Galatians, "…does God give you his Spirit and work miracles among you by the works of the law, or by your believing what you heard? So also Abraham 'believed God, and it was credited to him as righteousness.' Understand, then, that those who have faith are children of Abraham…

For all who rely on the works of the law are under a curse, as it is written: 'Cursed is everyone who does not continue to do everything written in the Book of the Law.' Clearly no one who relies on the law is justified before God, because 'the righteous will live by faith'" (Galatians 3:5-11).

This makes me think of something that Baptist preacher Robert Jeffress said in one of his sermons about the Christmas story (which is Jesus' birth). When word got out that the Savior was born, the religious leaders of that time and in that area heard about his birth, and they knew the prophecies, but not one of them traveled to see Jesus. I've heard it said that some of them were very close by and, yet, they still chose not to go see Jesus. As Robert Jeffress said, and I think it makes perfect sense, and again I'm paraphrasing, "they didn't care to come to Jesus because they didn't believe they needed a savior." They knew the law, they could recite it forward and backwards, they achieved the height of religious order and truly believed that their perceived good works toward the letter of the law was good enough to save them. They did the work, they held the titles, they reached the pinnacle, they did it themselves, therefore, they could save themselves through their own self-righteousness.

They did it themselves; they could save themselves; so why would they need a savior?

Makes sense to me, especially since they were some of the same ones who fought and argued with Jesus and sought His execution.

Little did they know, they, too, needed a savior.

The Messiah they had been waiting for to save them was the very same person they tried to cancel—the Person of Jesus was Jesus their Savior.

Through unbelief, people choose lies, they choose a life in sin, and they choose death.

The fallacy: if we can save ourselves, if we can atone for all our sins all on our own, if it was even possible to do more good works than bad in our lifetime and thus change the scales of judgment, then why would we need a savior? Why would we need Jesus? Why would we even need God? God, The Holy Spirit, Jesus, they would be irrelevant, obsolete, outdated, unworthy of our praise. In this case, we wouldn't need Christianity either; for the basis of Christianity is Jesus and the cross.

For it is **by your own hands** you have been **saved, through works**—and this is **not from God**, it is the **power of yourself** and your good works—by your own works, so that **you may boast.**

Is that not what Ephesians 2:8-9 says? We have saved ourselves so that we might boast of our own deeds and worthiness and self-righteousness?

No.

Is it true that a human priest can atone for our sins?

No.

Is it true that we must confess our sins to man, in private, and in a building which we call church, in order to be forgiven and saved?

No.

If we kill infidels (unbelievers) will we be saved and rewarded in Heaven?

No.

Remember the Ten Commandments?

So, what did Ephesians say?

Ephesians 2:8-9 says, "For it is *by grace* you have been *saved, through faith*—and this is *not from yourselves*, it is the *gift of God—not by works*, so that *no one can boast*."

"The law is not based on faith; on the contrary, it says, 'The person who does these things will live by them.' Christ redeemed us from the curse of the law by becoming a curse for us, for it is written: 'Cursed is everyone who is hung on a pole [tree—the crucifix].' He redeemed us in order that the blessing given to Abraham might come to the Gentiles [which is all of us, who were not and are not Jewish] through Christ Jesus, so that by faith we might receive the promise of the Spirit" (Galatians 3:12-14).

Jesus clearly said, "I am the way and the truth and the life. No one comes to the Father except through me" (John 14:6).

"If you declare [confess] with your mouth, 'Jesus is Lord,' and believe in your heart that God raised him from the dead, you will be saved" (Romans 10:9).

"For it is by grace you have been saved, through faith—and this is not from yourselves, it is the gift of God—not by works, so that no one can boast" (Ephesians 2:8-9).

If we could save ourselves through enough good works (deeds), confession to a pastor or priest, or rituals of religion, then we would not need God's gift of grace. If we did not need God, then there would be no need of Jesus; this would mean the birth, ministry, miracles, death, resurrection, faith, and saving grace would all be for nothing—it would all be a myth, a fable, a fairytale. For why does the world need God when the world can save itself?

In fact, if you listen to what the world says, it likes to claim that there are many paths to Heaven—in other words, they are saying there are many paths, many ways to be saved, and that all "truths" are truth and that all paths lead to Heaven. This is very interesting to me. Because if all "truths" are truth, then there really isn't any "truth" at all. To believe that all "truths" are truth, then you would need to believe in two opposing ideas, and that each are "truth." Or, as George Orwell very accurately described it in his book *1984*, "To know and to not know, to be conscious of complete truthfulness while telling carefully constructed lies, to hold simultaneously two opinions which cancelled out, knowing them to be contradictory and believing in both of them..."[10]

Remember: "No one can serve two masters. Either you will hate the one and love the other, or you will be devoted to the one and despise the other" (Matthew 6:24). And if you believe in Jesus, then you believe God's Word (that is, the Holy Bible) to be true—it is The Truth: "All Scripture is God-breathed and is useful for teaching, rebuking, correcting and training in righteousness" (2 Timothy 3:16).

It's also interesting to me because if all paths lead to Heaven, then why not live like Jane in the opening story of Chapter 4 and do whatever you want? Why not just enjoy yourself here on this earth since all paths lead to Heaven, and since all people, regardless of sin, regardless of choices, regardless of belief, regardless of faith, regardless of Jesus, regardless of God's Word, will go to Heaven?

For why does the world need God if the world can save itself?

But if you really pay attention, you will find that what the world is saying is not that all paths lead to Heaven or that all "truths" are truth, but, rather, the world is saying "there is only one 'truth,' the world's truth; there is only one way to Heaven, the world's way; and that there is only one Savior, the world."

God is the creator; Satan is the deceiver. God created all things; Satan can only warp, distort, confuse, and mutilate what God has created.

Think about it: Does the world silence Buddhism? Hinduism? Islam, which also claims there is only one way to Heaven, the rest are unbelievers (infidels) who will be thrown into Hell by their god? Well, maybe some countries cancel religion of most types, except political religion; and some cancel almost all gods, except themselves in power set as gods. Remember what I said earlier: the world is really saying, "there is only one 'truth.' the world's truth; there is only one way to Heaven, the world's way; and that there is only one Savior, the world."

No. In the super majority of cases, they silence one belief, they try to cancel the one way to Heaven, they try to get you and I to reject the one and only name: the only way, the only Truth, the only life; they silence, they try to cancel, Jesus our Savior.

If you have seen the movie *Do You Believe?*[11] then you will understand the power of this next part. If you haven't seen this movie, you should. It is really good. And the title is such a perfect question too: "Do You Believe?"

Anyway, in the movie, the character of Pastor Matthew gives a powerful sermon to his congregation while standing in front of a big cross. As he is talking, he wipes red paint on the cross, which symbolizes Jesus' blood.

He says to the congregation, "The cross is a gift. The greatest gift of all. It's forgiveness, redemption, new life. And it was paid for with blood."

Jesus' death upon the cross is our saving grace, and it was paid for with His blood.

Pastor Matthew continues saying, "Yet, when most of us look at the cross, we want the blood gone. We're ashamed of it. The blood that my sins—and yours— required as the price of our ransom."

We needed a savior, and God sent His only son to earth to bear all our sins and to die on that cross in our place so that we could be saved.

Our friend, the Person of Jesus, bore all our sins (1 Peter 2:24), He was beaten and battered, tortured, nailed to the cross, and He bled and died for you and I. Our friend sacrificed His life so you and I could have life eternal.

Romans 8:1 says, "Therefore, there is now no condemnation for those who are in Christ Jesus."

Jesus bore our sins; Jesus, who knew no sin, shed His own blood so that life could remain in ours; He took our place upon that cross—He took your place—and He suffered what should have been our death.

We needed a savior, for our path was death.

Jesus bore our sins… so that life could remain in ours.

The Person of Jesus—our friend—is Jesus our Savior.

Chapter 6:

Jesus our Sanctifier

"Sanctification is the real change in a man from the sordidness of sin to the purity of God's image."

William Ames[1]

Henry was a man of average build, but he was a man of true command; he was the CEO of a major corporation. He was on his way to work one morning when the trumpet sounded. He, along with all the other believers on earth, was immediately raptured up.

Now, here he is, standing in a crowd of billions, all gathered in front of the Pearly Gates.

"Henry!" a voice shouts amongst the crowd and chatter.

Henry looks around, slightly confused: Who shouted his name? How can he find them in this massive sea of people?

Henry turned all around, looking for the source of this voice.

"Henry!" the voice shouted again.

He turned around again and then he saw her—his wife. They were ecstatic and so thankful for God's blessing and love to have put all the couples near each other, even in the midst of this massive crowd, and to make sure that they all were reunited.

They embraced with the biggest hug they'd ever given each other, and they let out shouts of joy and shed tears of happiness.

A few moments later, the angel Gabriel appeared. He was standing right in front of the Pearly Gates.

Gabriel looked upon the crowd and shouted in a

voice loud enough that even those in the very back were able to clearly hear and understand his words, "I want all the men to form two lines," he said. "On the right side, I want all the men who were the true heads of their household. On the left side, I want all the men who allowed their wives to be the dominate heads of their household. And I want all the women to go see Mary on the other side of the gate!"

Henry and his wife thought, *this is very odd*, then they looked at each other and embraced once more.

Then, Henry said, "I guess I must get into line, and you need to go see Mary. I will see you inside."

He and his wife talked a few more moments and then he turned and headed toward his side, and she went to see Mary.

Once all the men were in their proper lines, Gabriel walked to the front of each line and looked back and forth between the left line and the right line, and he shook his head.

In the line on the left, with the men who were dominated by their wives, stood a line of men that seemed to extend into the horizon.

In the line on the right, with the men who were the dominant heads of their household, stood one man—Henry.

Gabriel looked toward all the men in the left line and said to them, "All of you should be ashamed of yourselves. You were all appointed to be the heads of your household. None of you in this line fulfilled what you were appointed to do in that area."

Then Gabriel looked at Henry; he stood alone in his line.

Gabriel said, "This is the only man who fulfilled his purpose with this appointment."

Henry smiled big; he was relishing in this moment.

Gabriel approached Henry and said, "Why don't you tell all the other men how you came to be standing in this line."

Henry looked at the men in the other line and shouted, "My wife told me to stand here!"[2]

Henry was set apart from all the other men.

Which brings us to sanctification.

What exactly is that word, sanctification? What does it mean?

For the longest time, I did not understand this word and the concept behind it. I was lost every time I heard someone preach or say that we are sanctified, and that Jesus is our sanctifier. I did not know what this word, sanctification, really meant.

You may be thinking a similar thing. But I assure you, you do know what it means, but just like me, you may not have known that it was this word that meant what you knew, and now know, that it means.

It is not a word I use in my everyday language; it is more of a "churchy" or "Christian-ese" word, you know. We use it to sound biblically literate and intelligent...

until someone asks us for more information on it, then we're just like, "You know, it's what Jesus did for us."

But did He? He died on the cross for us, to save us from our sins, but did Jesus completely sanctify us that day too?

So, I had to do more digging.

This is what I have found.

The word sanctify means "to set apart," "declaring something holy," "process of being freed from sin," and, "being purified."[3]

None of us can ever be perfect… But we are to repent, to change paths, and to look to our friend the Person of Jesus as our example of how to live while on this earth.

Are we set apart when we believe in Jesus and accept Him into our hearts as our Lord and Savior? Yes.

Are we declared holy by Jesus' sacrifice for us? Not yet.

Are we completed in our process of being freed from sin and purified? No.

Do I know what I am talking about? Well, let's read on and find out, shall we?

In the last chapter, we talked about death and sin: that death entered this world through sin, through Adam and Eve rejecting God's command and defying Him in the garden—their desire to know and be like God.

Defiance. Unbelief.

We talked about how until we can conquer sin, we will forever be unable to conquer death; until we conquer death, sin will rule.

To be fully sanctified, one must be purified—not partially, but fully purified—one must be set apart from sin, made holy (which is to be perfect—perfect in love, goodness and righteousness). However, no one can be sanctified if they are not first delivered or freed from sin. There can be no complete sanctification where there is still sin.

And since none of us are perfect— "for all have sinned and fall short of the glory of God" (Romans 3:23)—not one person (not you, or I) can ever be our own deliverers or free ourselves from sin. No person can be their own savior. Not even the world can save you.

Jesus said in John 14:6, "I am the way and the truth and the life. No one comes to the Father except through me."

Where is the Father? He is in Heaven. Yes, He's everywhere, God is omnipresent, but God the Father sits on His throne in Heaven. I'm not sure about you, but I want to be with the Father; I want to go to Heaven. And, as we've discussed, no amount of good works on our part could ever change the scales of judgment and save us and get us into Heaven. Only Jesus can. He is the only way.

And the only way to be holy is to be saved, forgiven, and fully sanctified. To conquer sin is to conquer death; to conquer death is to bring everlasting life. Our friend, the Person of Jesus, conquered death; Jesus conquered sin; Jesus brought everlasting life; Jesus is our Savior.

When you believe in Jesus and accept Him into your heart—not with just words or intellectual knowledge, but true faith, believing what you may not yet understand in God's Word—and you confess with your mouth that He is your Lord and Savior, then you will be saved.

When Jesus saves our lives, He brings life back to our Spirit, He writes Truth on our hearts, and He begins in us the process of sanctification so that we might work toward godliness while on this earth and present ourselves before God as sanctified, as Holy— His people set apart from the world. (Romans 12:2; Isaiah 43:1; Galatians 2:20; John 17:15-18; Ephesians 2:10; 1 Peter 1:16; Romans 12:1-2)

Now, no one can ever be perfect. Only Jesus was ever perfect. But we are to repent, to change paths, and to look to our friend the Person of Jesus as our example of how to live while on this earth.

"Do not conform to the pattern of this world, but be transformed…" (Romans 12:2).

When we accept Jesus, we are immediately set

apart; we are set apart from the world and adopted into the family of God. We are set apart as children of God. When we accept Jesus as our Lord and Savior, we are adopted into the family of God; we become heirs of God and His kingdom (Romans 8:14-17).

During the time that Paul wrote about this in Romans, the Roman Empire was the dominant empire in the world, and almost everyone understood what Paul was speaking of when he made the statements that those who were once slaves to sin were now adopted to sonship with "Abba, Father." Slaves had no rights, no inheritance; even freed slaves were considered to be not much better than those still in captivity, they were still considered less than worthy. In fact, I've been told by learned men of the Old Testament and the customs of the Jewish people in the Old Testament that in their customs back then, a son born into the family could be disowned, but a son adopted into the family could never be disowned. And, just as in the Roman Empire, when you were adopted, there was an expected change (or repentance) in your commitment and life. When you were adopted, you received a new lineage. With this adoption, the person being adopted became a family member in their new family, they became an heir. If you were adopted by a king (or, in that case, by an emperor), then you became an heir of their kingdom—you were set apart as a member of their lineage.

When we accept Jesus as our Lord and Savior, we become heirs to God, and as heirs, we receive the very same privileges and rights as a son to God—we are grafted into the vine of His chosen people, we are set apart as members of the lineage of the King of kings.

But, to be adopted means we were first in another life, another family, another lineage.

You will either defy God or defy Satan.

The word "testament" is the Greek translation for Covenant, which is a promise and often involves obligations and rituals. The Old Testament was God's covenant with His chosen people of Israel, which was bound by old rituals and sacrifices. The New Testament is God's covenant with all of humanity, which was bound by Jesus' sacrifice and secured by the shedding of Jesus' blood upon the cross. Our friend, the Person of Jesus, took our place upon that cross; our transgressions, our punishment—justice for our sins—was upon our friend the Person of Jesus as he made that cross a bridge for our salvation and became Jesus our Savior.

You are either with God or with Satan. You will either obey God or obey Satan. You will either defy God or defy Satan. You will either be saved by your acceptance and belief (your faith) through Jesus our Savior or you will be damned by your unbelief and rejection of God. It is all your own choice to make. We all have that choice, and we all must make that choice.

But once we are saved, and truly believe in Jesus with all our heart, then God dwells in us through the Holy Spirit, and by the Holy Spirit we are led to sanctification.

As Brody Jespersen says in his teachings, "sanctification is a life-long process." It is a life-long process of ours to choose so that we might live more like Christ, like the Person of Jesus, and be made holy.

And since sanctification is a life-long process, we will go through a process of being freed from sin, being purified, and growing in our Spirit.

Salvation is immediate, it is a life-changing, Spirit reviving, eye-opening, ear-heeding, soul exchanging, forever-changing, character growing, mind repainting, sanctification beginning, blessing by the grace of God.

But then the struggle between Spirit and Soul begins.

That is Sanctification—the process of being freed from sin; the process of being purified; the process of being made holy and presentable before God. It requires conscious and willful effort on our part. We must repent (change our thinking, change our ways, turn from the world and our selfishness and turn toward God and His Word) and begin building upon that new foundation.

Will we lose our salvation if we aren't perfect in our living sanctified? No, I do not believe so. However, you can choose to walk away from the blessings of God. For there are blessings that you miss in this life and often curses that you walk into by choosing to not obey God even if you truly believe in Jesus and confess. For sanctification is not complete until we pass from this life and into the next.

We have yet to be freed from sin. Yes, Jesus died on the cross for our sins, and He freed us from the curse of sin. When we believe in Him, we are freed from the curse of sin, which is death and eternal separation from God, but we are not freed from sin...yet.

Romans 12:2 (NLT) says, "Don't copy the behavior and customs of this world, but let God transform you into a new person by changing the way you think. Then you will learn to know God's will for you, which is good and pleasing and perfect."

"Do not conform to the pattern of this world," (NIV). Do not conform to this world; do not copy the behavior and customs of this world. Do not build your life on the foundation of this world.

"Do not be conformed to this world, but be transformed by the renewal of your mind, that by testing you may discern what is the will of God, what is good and acceptable and perfect" (ESV).

Joshua 1:8 says, "Keep this Book of the Law," that is the Holy Bible (not this book here, though it would be nice if you read this book many times). "Keep this Book of the Law always on your lips; meditate on it day and night, so that you may be careful to do everything written in it. Then you will be prosperous and successful."

"Our view of the world and ourselves will be shaped by and mirror the scent we hold in our minds."[4] What you feed yourself will begin to manifest in your life. If you feed yourself the behavior and customs of this world, then this world is whom you will begin to mirror, and this world will become your lineage. If you feed yourself the behavior and customs and Word of God, then Jesus is whom you will begin to mirror, and God's family will become your lineage.

"And do not be conformed to this world [any longer with its superficial values and customs], but be transformed *and* progressively changed [as you mature spiritually] by the renewing of your mind [focusing on godly values and ethical attitudes]" (Romans 12:12 AMP).

Jesus freed us from the everlasting, eternal furnace; He freed us from the second death; but we will not be freed from sin while we live in a sinful world and share space with a selfish soul.

Being totally freed from sin will not happen until we die. As long as we live on this earth, we will be tempted by sin, we will be fighting against the spiritual forces of darkness, we will have to make the choice, daily, as to whether we will feed the spirit or feed the soul.

"Keep this Book of the Law always on your lips; meditate on it day and night, so that you may be careful to do everything written in it. Then you will be prosperous and successful" (Joshua 1:8).

When we feed our spirit with The Truth (God's Word) and we spend time in prayer communicating with God and gather in assembly with other believers (Hebrews 10:24-25), we are being sanctified (we are taking action in the process of knowing, understanding, and growing in Christ), and through this we can then apply this spiritual growth in our lives and work toward living a Christ-like life.

We are saved by grace through faith in Christ Jesus (Ephesians 2:8).

Or, we can choose to feed our soul, go our own way, seek our own desires, appease our own will, and give into our emotional flesh, moving further away from God's calling, God's desire for our lives, God's will, God's love for us, and live a life separated from God.

"In the same way, faith by itself, if it is not accompanied by action, is dead" (James 2:17).

In either choice, we will be set apart: apart from the world or apart from God.

When we are saved, we are born again; when we are born again, we are babies in Christ. Our spirit is born again and it is like a baby, needing guidance and sustenance. As babies, we, "Like newborn babies, crave pure spiritual milk, so that by it you may grow up in your salvation, now that you have tasted that the Lord is good" (1 Peter 2:2-3).

That is us when we are born again—we are different in nationality and physical appearance, but we are all children of God, and we are all seeking the pure spiritual milk of God's Word so that our spirit might grow and, as we grow, the Holy Spirit can then guide us further in the process of sanctification.

No matter how old we are spiritually, every one of us, although we are freed from the curse of sin, are yet freed from sin; we can still backslide, we can still live a life in sin, shrinking in spirit, and once again require milk for sustenance. We all have free will to choose for ourselves what we will feed ourselves, whom we will serve, and how we will live. That is why it is so important to renew our mind every day, to not forsake the assembling of believers, to pray and communicate with God every day, and to seek to grow spiritually. We must make that effort to seek God and to understand His Word and plan for our lives.

Hebrews 5:11-14 says, "We have much to say about this, but it is hard to make it clear to you because you no longer try to understand. In fact, though by this time you ought to be teachers, you need someone to teach you the elementary truths of God's Word all over again. You need milk, not solid food! Anyone who lives on milk, being still an infant, is not acquainted with the teaching about righteousness. But solid food is for the mature, who by constant use have trained themselves to distinguish good from evil."

What he is talking about comes through sanctification, which is only possible by our choice to willingly seek God and His Word—really, it will be a daily fight to keep our soul in check and allow the Spirit to lead.

"Ask and it will be given to you; seek and you will find; knock and the door will be opened to you" (Matthew 7:7).

In Mark 9:14-29, we see a large crowd gathered around the disciples, and in this crowd is a father who brought his son directly to Jesus to be healed; the boy was demon possessed since childhood. He went to Jesus and asked Jesus, "…if you can…" to which Jesus replied, "Everything is possible for one who believes." Then, we see in verse 24, the father says a profound statement, "I do believe; help me overcome my unbelief."

When we accept Jesus as our savior, we are repeating the first part of this man's reply, "I do believe." But then comes the sanctification process where we continue to seek God's guidance, through the Holy Spirit, in the name of Jesus, and throughout this process of sanctification, God helps us "overcome our unbelief"; that is, He continues to help us grow and mature in our spiritual life.

There is a great quote from a daily devotional that is based on the movie *Do You Believe?* that reads, "Spiritual growth is like a plant. You can take a look at any plant of any type and make a judgment call on whether it is thriving or dying. The appearance of the leaves, branches, or blooms give us clues. Is it reaching upward, showing health and growth, or wilting downward in distress? But is a plant ever just in a state of neutrality, not growing or dying? No, it is always heading in one direction or the other. The same is true for our spiritual growth."[5]

As we have mentioned previously, God is the creator, Satan is the destroyer. God has given each one of us the authority and free will to choose whom we will serve. In doing so, we will have the opportunity to either create or destroy: opportunities, growth, maturity, hope, and life.

I've heard this preached many times, and it lines up well with what we were talking about when it comes to our soul and spirit: the younger leading the older is a prevalent prophecy in the Old Testament, which explains well the spiritual battle for each individual in the New Testament.

Jacob and Esau: Genesis 25:23, "…and the older will serve the younger."

Romans 9:12, "The older will serve the younger."

Joseph and his brothers (Genesis 37 – Genesis 50).

Your soul is the older, since it was in charge from the time you were born. Until you were of age, your soul ruled.

But once you became of age and accepted Jesus into your heart, your spirit became alive; you were born again. When your spirit became alive, it told the soul that it was now in charge, and your soul, being the selfish desires of your will, mind and emotions, said, "over my dead body."

When you allow your soul to lead, when you only feed your soul and reject God and the spirit, then your soul gets its desire: "over my dead body"—your destiny is death. But if you feed your spirit with God's Word and allow the Holy Spirit to work in you and your life (sanctification), then your destiny will be life.

The older shall serve the younger. Sanctification is a process that lasts throughout our life.

Just as our bodies and minds grow in this natural world, so will our spirit. And just like our bodies will be affected by what we feed it in the natural, and our minds will be affected by what we feed it through what we watch, read, listen to, and think about—meditate on—so shall our spirit be affected by what we feed it, or, in the absence of God, how much we choose to starve it.

In either choice, we will be set apart: apart from the world or apart from God.

If we choose God, then we are declared holy in the presence of the Lord when our sanctification is complete.

Are you ready for the catch here? It was mentioned earlier, but it is a hard concept to accept in the beginning.

Sanctification is not completed until we are dead.

As long as we are in the presence of sin, sanctification will never be complete.

It is upon our crossing of this life and into the next, through grace in faith and by the blood of Jesus Christ, that we are fully sanctified before the Lord, and thus, by the righteousness of Jesus, we are fully freed from sin, purified, and made holy.

The Person of Jesus is our friend and our example of character on this earth. The Person of Jesus gave His life so that we might have life everlasting; and in doing so, He became Jesus our Savior. The Person of Jesus, our friend, became Jesus our Savior, who, with the Holy Spirit, became Jesus our Sanctifier.

Chapter 7:

Jesus our Healer

"What we consider to be miraculous is everyday life for God. Nothing is impossible for Him."

Cindy M. Carpenter[1]

There were three men who all claimed to know God and love Jesus.

James was a first responder who had a horrific accident while saving Hank's life. James broke his back and became paralyzed from the waist down, and he is now confined to a wheelchair. James sacrificed his life for another to be saved (John 15:13). He attends church every week, living up to the Scripture as it states in Hebrews 10:24-25, "And let us consider how we may spur one another on toward love and good deeds, not giving up meeting together, as some are in the habit of doing, but encouraging one another…"

Brad is an insurance agent, and he was the one who helped file the claims for both James and Hank. He spent most of his time, years in fact, hunched over piles of paperwork and claims. He developed bad forward head posture and a hunchback; as his spine developed a bad curve from this poor posture, it began to pinch his nerves, and his neck and back began to cause him a lot of pain, and he took pain pills to ease this pain. Brad sacrificed hours of his life to help those who were injured. He lived by 1 John 3:17 (ESV), "But if anyone has the world's goods and sees his brother in need, yet closes his heart against him, how does God's love abide in him?" However, he took it to the extreme.

Hank was the young man who James saved and whom Brad helped because he was injured. Hank never stayed in one job too long; he was always looking for the next quick and easy buck. Hank trusted in his own wits and cunning, never thinking much about anyone but himself—his own well-being. He never attended church and he didn't read his Bible. He believed that he was saved and therefore he didn't need church or God's laws or wisdom in his life; he didn't want to change his ways, and he believed he could save and help himself. He was unaware of this, but he lived his life by the wisdom of the world, like it states in Colossians 2:8 (NET), "Be careful not to allow anyone to captivate you through an empty, deceitful philosophy that is according to human traditions and the elemental spirits of the world, and not according to Christ." Hank had a knowledge of Jesus, but he had no faith and did not truly believe in Jesus.

One day, James wheeled himself into the local diner and asked the waitress for a cup of coffee. As he did, he noticed a person, who looked very familiar to him, sitting at the end of the counter, alone, and praying.

James asked the waitress, "Is that Jesus over there?"

The Waitress said, "Yes, it is."

James then told her to pour Jesus a cup of coffee, on him.

A few moments later, Brad shuffled into the diner and painfully sat in a booth. He ordered a cup of hot tea from the same waitress, and then he, too, noticed Jesus sitting at the counter.

Brad asked her, "That man over there, is that Jesus?"

She said, "Yes, it is."

Brad ordered a cup of hot tea and told the waitress to bring it to Jesus, on him.

Next, Hank hobbled in on crutches. He sat at a table, ordered a soda, and then he, too, noticed Jesus.

He asked the same question to the same waitress, "Is that Jesus over there?"

She said, "Yes, it is."

Hank took out his wallet, looked inside it, and pulled out a fifty-dollar bill.

He looked at the waitress and said, "I've finally got money. God's finally come through; well, I had to do the work, and it cost me, but by my own cunning and deeds, I've finally come into a lot of money. I'm so clever. So, with this money here, I want to buy Jesus whatever he wants to eat. It's the least I can do. Take it to him and make sure he knows this is from me. I will take care of him."

The waitress did just as Hank asked.

When Jesus was done eating and drinking, He got up to leave. As He did, He passed by James first and touched him. James was immediately healed. He jumped up from his wheelchair and danced around the diner, praising God for his healing.

Then Jesus walked by Brad and touched him. He, too, was immediately healed. Brad stood up, lifted his hands, looked up toward heaven, and began praising God, too.

Then Jesus walked up to Hank and reached out

to touch him, but Hank immediately jumped back, swatting Jesus' hand away.

Hank screamed at Jesus, "Don't touch me! I'm collecting disability!"[2]

There is nothing you have done that can separate you from the love of God.

How many times do we show kindness and knowledge in Jesus, but then deny him access to our very lives? Maybe it's because we value earthly possessions or sympathy from others more than we value Him; or in our self-centeredness or fear we foolishly believe God's healing power would be a detriment to us because we can take care of ourselves, we don't need His healing, or because, like Hank, we think His miracle would be detrimental to what we currently have and we suffered to get what we currently have. Maybe we believe that we are not worthy of His healing touch. Maybe we just do not believe that He does miracles or healing like that anymore. Or, we might think we deserve the pain or sickness or whatever it might be because of our sin.

How many times have we told Jesus "don't touch me! Don't touch me and my life" by our lack of faith? Our Fear? Our death grip on what little we have or our current complacent life? Our worry of what the world might think of us? Our feeling that we deserve less than God's perfect love and grace and power and healing? Or by our fear that what we have might be the best we will ever get or have?

I tell you, the best decision I have made apart from believing in Jesus is letting go and letting Him take control. I did this with my career. I held so tightly to being a known filmmaker and contract media worker that I was too afraid to step out of the current role I was in and let God lead me—my identity had become planted in what I did rather than who God says I am. Once I let go of it, God led me to the completion of so many goals (many I hadn't had a previous desire to even think about), win awards, write multiple books, become a teacher, and do many things that I could never have dreamed of before—things that help prove the saying, "God equips the called." That's how these books came to be. He put this passion and desire in my heart; it was something I had to do, and something I really wanted to do, but not until I let go and let God. I've also done this with my finances. For nearly two decades I clung to the dollar—it was all about the Benjamins… well, Washington's, really—focusing mostly on how much a place or client would pay me rather than just doing the absolute best job I could and watching God provide. I still did the best I could because it's something my dad engrained in his children, but it was more out of a nagging obligation than complete work ethic and trust. But when I began to let go and focus on God first, He began to work mightily and healing of my mind, soul, and emotions began to take root.

We must allow Jesus to touch our lives.

"Who shall separate us from the love of Christ? Shall trouble or hardship or persecution or famine or nakedness or danger or sword? As it is written: 'For your sake we face death all day long; we are considered as sheep to be slaughtered.' No, in all these things we are more than conquerors through him who loved us. For I am convinced that neither death nor life, neither angels nor demons, neither the present nor the future, nor any powers, neither height nor depth, nor anything else in all creation, will be able to separate us from the love of God that is in Christ Jesus our Lord" (Romans 8:35-39).

There is nothing you have done, past or present, that can separate you from the love of God. God loves you no matter what; He is just waiting for you to accept Him and to love Him back. Trust the physician and let Him heal you.

How can you receive when your hands are still full?

Jesus already died for our sins; He is our Savior because He freed us from the curse of sin—death, eternal separation from God, sickness, these are all curses of sin. He is our Sanctifier because He is working in us, and, if we allow Him, He is working through us. But we must allow Jesus to touch our lives. We must not shrink back and we must not avoid His touch, His calling.

In Mark 10:13-16 we see that people were bringing their children to Jesus so that He might touch them and bless them. "People were bringing little children to Jesus for him to place his hands on them, but the disciples rebuked them."

"Don't touch them," was the disciple's response—those closest to Jesus, those who were walking with Jesus, being taught directly by Jesus, those who claimed to love Jesus and want to be like Jesus. Those who were freed from the curse of sin, were still living in a world with sin, and, therefore, they still battled with sin in their lives. Sanctification is a process.

But why did the disciples demand that people not touch Jesus? Was Jesus only able to give a limited supply of blessings? Of miracles? Of healing? Is that why we can sometimes pray and pray and pray and feel like we do not see God working anywhere in our lives, healing our loved ones, repairing our nation, fixing our problems? Because God's supply is low or there is a limited quantity, and He must use it sparingly?

We have all fallen into this mind-trap of the enemy, I'm sure. "God, I prayed, I've brought my petition to you, I've quoted your own words of blessing, healing, and prosperity over my life, where are you? Where is your working hand? Where is my healing?"

How little patience, how little perseverance, how little faith we must have sometimes. Then again, maybe we are too time conscious and expect God to move on our time schedule. I've been there many times.

I have brought this same question before God, not solely about healing, but about finances. I have said, "God, I've followed you, I've been doing what you want me to do even when I don't understand why or see the vision for the end yet (with the occasional mindset of a rebellious teenager, but I've followed you). Where is the green pasture? Where is the light? Where is the evidence that you are working? Where is my promised land?" And you know what I felt He told me: "Patience. Hold firm to your faith in Me. Keep going, step by step, where I lead. You cannot see everything, but I am working. My timing is not the world's timing, nor is it your timing. But my timing is worth everything."

That did bring some peace in that moment, but it wasn't long before the battle in my mind began to rage again; and whenever I've given ground there, every aspect of my body and life began to feel the impact of that compromise. It's hard to hold firm when the hurricane winds of life are blowing tidal waves on your emotions. It's hard to keep taking steps forward when you feel like every step forward with God is being countered by life pushing you three steps back? It's hard to accept God's timing when you can't see or in that moment even feel the fulness of God's promise and blessings. But trust me, it is worth it. There is freedom in the name of Jesus; there is peace in the end; God is working behind the scenes; God is preparing you; there is healing. For more than a decade I felt that—the pain, the ache, the struggle, the love, the promise, the peace. In the end, it was all worth it; God's timing was the best timing; God kept His word and fulfilled the promise.

Mark 10 continues by saying, "When Jesus saw this," that is, when Jesus saw His disciples rebuking the children, "he was indignant. He said to them, 'Let the little children come to me, and do not hinder them, for the kingdom of God belongs to such as these. Truly I tell you, anyone who will not receive the kingdom of God like a little child will never enter it.' And he took the children in his arms, placed his hands on them and blessed them."

The disciples rebuked the people; they rebuked the children. Jesus said, "…anyone who will not receive the kingdom of God like a child…"

What did He mean by that?

He meant, I think, that children have yet to understand or be blinded by a feeling of legality, a feeling that they were deserving of a free gift like Grace. They were still innocent and considered pure. A child is considered innocent and pure until they become of age; an age where they can begin to understand the concepts of right and wrong, and, thus, be accountable for their own belief or unbelief. As adults, we can sometimes feel that we deserve things from God, that we are entitled to His blessings, and that God owes us, when the reality is, we do not deserve anything, except His judgment; and I don't know about you, but I do not want God's judgment to fall upon me, I want His grace and mercy—it is by Grace, by God's love for us, that we are able to be saved, and it is by this same love from God, His grace and mercy, that we receive healing.

Jesus called you; He loves you.

Our good works will not earn us salvation, nor will they earn us any more love or grace or mercy from God. He already loves us with all His heart; He already gave us all authority by the sacrifice of His son, Jesus, and Jesus' resurrection and conquering of sin and death. God already loves you (Romans 5:8); Your life, human life, is valuable (Matthew 6:26); God has made you justified (1 Corinthians 6:11); You are worthy and your identity is in Him (1 Corinthians 6:17; Genesis 1:27; 1 Corinthians 12:27; 1 Peter 2:9).

It is a gift from God that we have the authority, in the name of Jesus, to pray for and command healing.

Matthew 10 says, "Jesus called his twelve disciples to him and gave them…"

Jesus called them; He loved them. Jesus called you; He loves you. Jesus did not charge them, He did not demand that they earn it, it was not something even the disciples were entitled to, it was a gift. Jesus gave them…Jesus gives you…

He "gave them authority to drive out impure spirits and to heal every disease and sickness" (Matthew 10:1).

In Matthew 10:8, Jesus told them to "Heal the sick, raise the dead, cleanse those who have leprosy, drive out demons."

And they did so because they deserved this power and authority; it was their entitlement because they earned it, they did enough good works to earn enough points to purchase this power from God's ticket counter; they received it because God owed them, right?

NO!

Jesus said to "Heal the sick…[because] Freely you

have received; freely give" (Matthew 10:8).

This power, this authority, to heal the sick and to drive out demons, was freely given, it is a gift from God to those who believe in Jesus; because this power and authority is derived, not from us, not from our deserving right, not from our good works, but from the name of Jesus—the very same Jesus who freely gave His life for yours.

Romans 13:1 says (ESV) "…For there is no authority except from God…"

If you believe in Jesus, then this same authority has been freely given to you; all you have to do is to freely receive it.

But, how can you receive when your hands are still full? How can you receive when your hands are clenched in a fist? How can you receive when your hands are stuck in the muck of past regrets and sins?

It is difficult to receive a gift if you feel you are not worthy of such a gift, and it is difficult, no, impossible to wield such power if you feel you are entitled to and deserving of God's power because of your own self-righteousness.

Because God loved you (He loves each of us) so much, He gave His Son to suffer our judgment and to free us from the curse of sin.

Jesus, by His sacrifice, made you worthy; God, by His grace, gave you the authority to use the power in the name of His Son, Jesus. It is not by our power or by our might, but by His, and all praise and worship are God's.

In Matthew 28:18: Jesus said, "All authority in heaven and on earth has been given to me."

Mark 16:17-18 says, "And these signs will accompany those who believe: In my name they will drive out demons; they will speak in new tongues… they will place their hands on sick people, and they will get well."

Luke 10:19 says, "I have given you authority to trample on snakes and scorpions and to overcome all the power of the enemy…"

The very same power and authority that the disciples had is the very same power and authority that I have and that you have—it is the very same power and authority that every believer has. If it was the power and authority to heal the sick by the deserving right, or entitlement, of the disciples, then that power and authority would be long gone…unless each of us did whatever the human ritual was that was the power and authority of man by which the disciples cast out demons and healed the sick.

If it was power and authority of man, then it was already doomed and corrupted; and it held no more authority than a blind referee, and no more power than a new-born baby in a strong-man competition.

What they had was the power and authority in the one and only name, and by the only person to live without sin, to live with a perfect character, and that is Jesus; the very same name that gives us, each believer today, the power and authority to heal the sick.

There is power in the name of Jesus!

Pastor Brody Jespersen says that there are three points to fully tapping into this power, and each one deals with prayer. Part of our sanctification process is building our prayer life. Prayer is our greatest communication channel with God, and this channel was built by Jesus and paved by His beaten, bruised and sacrificed body so that each one of us could have that personal relationship with our Heavenly Father.

"…he was pierced for our transgressions, he was crushed for our iniquities; the punishment that brought us peace was on him, and by his wounds we are healed" (Isaiah 53:5).

We are healed, but it is up to us to accept this gift.

It is always our choice.

And that brings us to the three points, as Brody mentions in his course "Who Is Jesus?"

Point 1: Pray with Confidence.

Matthew 21:22 (ESV) says, "And whatever you ask in prayer, you will receive, if you have faith."

Faith, I like to say, is complete trust and confidence.

God says in 1 Corinthians 2:5 (ESV), "That your faith might not rest in the wisdom of men but in the power of God."

It is not a matter of if, for God can. Jesus said in Mark 9:23, "Everything is possible for one who believes."

However, we must also understand that just because we do not see an immediate answer, that does not mean God is not working.

Healing might not always be instant; it could be gradual, a process, just like sanctification. But even so, we should hold on to our faith and belief in the power of the name of Jesus and the authority by which God gave us, that, in His time and by His will, that healing will be complete.

It can sometimes be hard to continue to hold on to faith when we think we do not see God moving or working, especially when we think we know better and that our understanding of timing is more powerful than God's, but that is another reason we need to renew our minds in God's Word. I do believe that is also where God's love and grace and mercy for us is at work once again. Jesus said, in Matthew 17:20, "Because you have so little faith. Truly I tell you, if you have faith as small as a mustard seed, you can say to this mountain, 'Move from here to there,' and it will move. Nothing will be impossible for you."

Why?

Because the power is not in us, it is not in our ability or our spiritual level of growth, or our rain forest sized faith, it is solely in Jesus, and by our faith in Him (even as small as a mustard seed), Jesus can work miracles.

I mean, without faith we have no hope, and without hope, we are no better off than a one-armed man in a swimming contest. Sure, some people will claim he is swimming laps around his opponents, but in reality, he is just going around in a never ending, depressing, hopeless, joyless, and powerless circle until he eventually gives up and drowns.

So, we are to pray with confidence that God will hear us and that the authority granted to us by the power in the name of Jesus will be answered.

To reaffirm our faith in prayer, and to increase it, we should not skip point two.

Point 2: Pray With Others.

"For where two or three gather in my name, there am I with them" (Matthew 18:20).

To pray with others is to be honest about your need and to seek help or guidance.

You have not because you ask not (James 4:2-3).

When we pray to God, we are having a discussion with God, we are communicating with God, and, in doing so, we can then ask God for His help, for His healing.

When we pray with others, we are not only letting others know what we know—without us telling them, people don't always know—but we are also accomplishing what the Lord said: "Carry each other's burdens, and in this way you will fulfill the law of Christ" (Galatians 6:2). Praying with others also invites us to seek the needs of others and to encourage each other.

And when we pray with confidence, and when we pray with others, we should always pray in the name of Jesus.

Point 3: Pray In The Name Of The Lord

John 14:13-14 (NKJV) says, "Whatever you ask in my name [in the name of Jesus], that I will do, that the Father may be glorified in the Son."

It is all about the glorification of God, not our ability to pray or heal. It is all about God, and God is glorified when people see and experience healing in the name of His Son Jesus.

But we must, as Point 1 stated, pray with confidence.

"And this is the confidence that we have toward him, that if we ask anything according to his will he hears us" (1 John 5:14 ESV).

We have been given the authority to heal.

Jesus clearly said, in John 14:12, "Very truly I tell you, whoever believes in me will do the works I have been doing, and they will do even greater things than these, because I am going to the Father."

Jesus healed the sick, the lame, the diseased, the blind, the deaf, the demon possessed, the spiritual, mental, physical and emotional sicknesses in people; Jesus even raised the dead. And here He is, clearly telling us—all who believe in Him—that we, too, will do the very same works that He did while walking this earth, and we will do even greater works!

Jesus is our Healer, but He is also our power by which we, too, are granted the authority to lay hands on the hurting, the lost, the sick, and heal them by the power of God in the name of Jesus Christ.

There is no other name than the name of Jesus.

The Person of Jesus, our friend, died for our sins and became Jesus our Savior.

Jesus our Savior filled that chasm that separated us from a personal relationship with God, our Father, and began in us the process of sanctification.

Jesus our Sanctifier, through the Holy Spirit, by the grace and power of God, gave us the authority to heal in His name.

He gave us the authority to show the world that Jesus is Our Healer.

Chapter 8:

Jesus our coming King & Living Missionally

"A king without power is an absurdity."

James Monroe[1]

"He [the king] sat atop his golden chair, observing those who were commissioned to build him his empire. He had distinction that set him apart from the front-line worker, which, as he interpreted for himself, was every person beneath his command, and this distinction meant he was in charge."[2]

The world saw him by his title; to the world, one's identity was what they did, or in this case, what they had accepted as the "divine right" of heritage. To them, your heritage, what is acquired from a predecessor, was more important than your family lineage. Your heritage meant you inherited something (a right or title) by law when your ancestor died—if they were royalty, then, if you were next in line, you received the crown and the earthly power that came with that inheritance. It was a divine right by law; but it only applied to one person—by law, by birth. Because of this, they ignored Galatians 3:13, Galatians 3:25, and Romans 6:14 and also ignored one's lineage. All of which would apply to those adopted and no longer under the curse of the law, they had a new family, a new inheritance for all, and all were heirs—as in, adopted into the family lineage of Christ (Galatians 4:5; Romans 8:15).

"His status made him appear superior; he held influence to ensure his demands were met; he had a white-knuckled grip on the power to punish any person who disobeyed...he was king."[3]

He was a king who thought only of himself and his personal desires. He was so vain and prideful that he could only think of the current—the desire of the day; and he would punish anyone who failed him, for any reason. He was the ruler of this world.

Well, one day, one of his servants gave him some advice, which, as time went on, was proven to be the wrong advice for that situation. This wrong advice did not cost the king anything of earthly value, and most of his subjects never even noticed, but what it did do was cost him a moment of his pride. So, in his anger and egocentric narcissism, he ordered this servant to be thrown into a pit where his twelve wild and vicious dogs were kept. He was going to enjoy watching this servant suffer the gnashing of teeth and being torn apart, alive.

As the servant was being dragged from the king's presence by the king's guards, he shouted, "Why are you doing this? I have served you loyally and correctly for more than ten years?"

The king shouted to his guards, "Stop!" He looked toward the servant and said, "You failed me. Today you shall die."

The servant pleaded with the king, "Please, your majesty, give me ten days, just ten days, before you throw me into the pit to be eaten alive by your dogs? After that, do what you will. But grant your servant this one request, please."

The king paused, contemplating this request for a moment. Then he thought to himself, *This is a great opportunity for the people to see me as a gracious king while I still get to watch this man die.* So, the king agreed.

The servant immediately left the kings presence and went to see the keeper of the dogs.

He asked the keeper of the dogs, "Sir, I only have ten days left before I am sentenced to die. May I please spend my last days serving you and the dogs?"

The keeper was confused by this odd request, but he liked this man's willingness to serve the king until his last breath. So, he said, "Yes."

During those ten days, the servant fed, watered, washed, played with, and cared for those dogs like they were his own, like they were family.

When the ten days were up, the servant was brought before the king who ordered that he be immediately thrown to the dogs, as per his sentence.

When the servant was thrown into the pit with the dogs, everyone, including the king, were shocked and amazed—the servant was not harmed. The dogs ran around him, jumped on him, licked him, and were wagging their tails, happy to see their friend; there was no sign of the viciousness that was present in these dogs just ten days prior.

The king angrily demanded, "What happened to those dogs?!"

The servant looked at the king and declared, "For only ten days, I served these dogs loyally, and they did not forget my service. And yet, for over ten years I served you loyally and you forgot all my loyalty in one moment, at the sign of my very first mistake. There was no grace, no mercy, no love, no forgiveness from you, just judgment and death in your court. These dogs have shown more mercy today than you have shown in your lifetime."

Everyone in attendance hushed and looked toward the king. The king hung his head and realized his mistake.

He, then, looked up and shouted, "Take those dogs out of the pit, and replace them crocodiles!"[4]

Every kingdom has a king.

Every kingdom has a king. And we all will live in one kingdom, and we all will serve one king.

I don't know about you, but I do not want to serve a king who is only out for himself, and who only uses me for his own wicked purposes. I want to serve a King who is looking out for me, one whom I can "Take delight in…and he will give you the desires of your heart" (Psalm 37:4).

I do not want to serve a king who knows nothing of grace and mercy; I do not want to serve a king who does not forgive, but only gets even. I want to serve a King who freely offers grace and mercy for those who accept it; I want to serve a King who forgives me and one who will "remember me and care for me. Avenge me on my persecutors" (Jeremiah 15:15).

I do not want to serve a king who wants death for me; I do not want to serve a king who will throw me to the dogs for my mistakes. I want to serve a King who says, "If you repent, I will restore you…I will make you a wall to this people, a fortified wall of bronze; they will fight against you but will not overcome you, for I am with you to rescue and save you" (Jeremiah 15:19-20).

I do not want to serve a king who is the father of lies; I do not want to serve a king whose desire is to drag me down to the pits, thrown to the dogs, and to live in agony and torment for eternity. I want to serve a King who is the Truth and life (John 14:6); I want to serve a king whose desire for me is to have eternal life (John 3:16, Romans 6:23), to have peace (John 16:33), wisdom and knowledge and understanding (Proverbs 2:6, James 1:5, James 3:17), to be set apart from death, pain, and sadness (Revelation 21:4), to be free (Galatians 3:13).

I do not want to serve a king whose concept of love is to be blind to wickedness, to sin, and to reject God's Word; I do not want to serve a king whose idea of love is that I die to serve their selfish desires. I want to serve a King who is perfect in love, peace, and righteousness, and who showers me with grace; I want to serve a King whose love sees all my mess and mistakes and still chooses to love me (1 Peter 4:8); I want to serve a King who is love (1 John 4:16); I want to serve a King who is and shows me love (John 3:16).

I do not want to serve a king who desires to see my death. I want to serve a King who "demonstrates his own love for us in this: While we were still sinners, Christ died for us" (Romans 5:8).

A quote I heard from a movie (I think it was one of the Halo movies but I do not remember which one for sure), and I think it is worth ruminating on, is: "Will your life bring death, or will your death bring life?"

Our Friend is our Savior and our Sanctifier in whom we have the authority to use His name to be Jesus our Healer.

And all this is granted because "All authority in heaven and on earth has been given to [Jesus]" (Matthew 28:18).

"The Lord will be king over the whole earth. On that day there will be one Lord, and his name the only name" (Zechariah 14:9).

Jesus took the keys of death and the grave; Jesus took back the authority on this earth from Satan; Jesus holds the keys and the authority and the power (Revelation 1:18).

"For the Lord is our judge, the Lord is our lawgiver, the Lord is our king…" (Isaiah 33:22).

"Then I saw 'a new heaven and a new earth,' for the first heaven and the first earth had passed away…" (Revelation 21:1).

Jesus said, "…no one can see the kingdom of God unless they are born again" (John 3:3). And to be born again, you must accept Jesus as your Lord and Savior.

Every kingdom has a king.

We all live in one kingdom; we will all plant our values and our standards in one foundation, and we will all build our castles on one type of foundation (Matthew 7:24-27); and we will all serve one king.

The question is: Whose kingdom do you choose to live in? This will determine who you will call king.

"But if serving the Lord seems undesirable to you, then choose for yourselves this day whom you will serve…in whose land you are living. But as for me and my household, we will serve the Lord" (Joshua 24:15).

My friend, Jesus, who lives in me, is my identity—He is my King. I pray that you, too, will choose Jesus as your King, and that you, too, will realize your true identity is in Jesus, not in your title, or bank account, or career, or any other thing this world tries to noose you with. If your identity is anchored in your King, Jesus Christ, then your anchor, your foundation, will hold firm through any storm (Colossians 2:5; Isaiah 41:10-13).

Therefore, we live in the kingdom of God and that is why we can say Jesus Is Our Coming King.

And how do we serve our King? How do we live missionally?

By choosing to give our life to Him; by choosing to live in His kingdom; by choosing to live under the will of our King; by choosing to love Him who first loved us (1 John 4:19), and by sharing our King's good news to all whom He loves, which is all people—by spreading His Gospel, His love, His open invitation for saving grace and redemption, and by being his "witnesses…to the ends of the earth" (Acts 1:8).

Whose kingdom do you choose to live in?

Chapter 9:

Conclusion

"Here I am! I stand at the door and knock. If anyone hears my voice and opens the door, I will come in and eat with that person, and they with me."

Revelation 3:20[1]

Jesus appeared to many people after His death and resurrection, and He did so with holes in His hands and the wound in His side—marks of a wounded body, a PERSON'S body. The Person of Jesus.

Jesus is our friend; and you cannot have a personal relationship unless they are a person; therefore, we discussed the Person of Jesus.

Remember this, if you look up "personal relationships" you will find these as the examples of having a personal relationship with someone:

- Companionship

- Intimacy

- Love

- Friendship

- Solidarity

- Trust

It is the Person of Jesus who is our friend, whom we can, and do, have a personal relationship with—we trust Him, love Him, are solidified in Him, and He walks beside us in companionship.

If you love Jesus, if you trust Jesus, if you build that friendship with Jesus, then you are doing so with the Person of Jesus.

And it is the Person of Jesus who demonstrates to us a godly character by which we can and should aspire to emulate in our lives.

Our friend loves us; and we have the free will to choose to love Him who first loved us.

As Philip Yancey states in his book *Disappointment with God*, "In a concentration camp...the guards possess nearly unlimited power. By applying force, they can make you renounce your God, curse your family...kill... All this is within their power. Only one thing is not: they cannot force you to love them."[2]

For God so loved the world that your friend willingly stood in your place and sacrificed Himself to save you!

There is no other thing on this earth that cannot be forced or coerced or controlled by fear.

"There is no fear in love. But perfect love drives out fear..." (1 John 4:18).

Love is a gift, it is a choice. And since our friend was perfect, He is perfect love; therefore, our friend willingly stood in our place and sacrificed Himself to save us.

"There is no greater love than to lay down one's life for one's friends" (John 15:13 NLT).

Therefore, our friend, the Person of Jesus, became Jesus our Savior.

Then we talked about Jesus our Savior.

There was and is only one person who can save us, and that person is Jesus; He is Jesus our Savior.

Romans 5:12 (NKJV) says, "Therefore, just as through one man sin entered the world, and death through sin, and thus death spread to all men, because all sinned…"

Death, disease, sickness, pain, mental illness, emotional distress, confusion, and a lost identity—all entered through sin when Adam and Eve first sinned in the Garden of Eden. We chose death, but our friend stepped in, stood before the Great Judge, and took our punishment for our sins (Romans 3:23-26).

The Person of Jesus suffered our judgment on that cross for our sins—He died with the weight of our sins. By doing so, He became the sacrificial lamb by which we are saved (in those times, only a firstborn, male lamb without defect was worthy to be offered as a sacrifice—Jesus was the firstborn, male without defect worthy to be offered as a sacrifice for you and I); and not only are we saved from the curse of sin (if we believe in Him and accept Him in our hearts), but Jesus also defeated death and the grave; Jesus took the keys of death and the authority that Adam foolishly handed over to Satan on this earth, and He, through the Holy Spirit, imparted each one of us—every believer—with all the authority in the power of His name.

In Matthew 28:18, Jesus said, "All authority in heaven and on earth has been given to me…"

Jesus defeated sin; He defeated the grave and death; He defeated Satan; He is victory.

The Person of Jesus, our friend, is always with us, and He is Jesus our Savior.

But He loved us so much that He imparted in us the Holy Spirit.

Our Friend became Our Savior who, with the help of the Holy Spirit, became Jesus our Sanctifier.

Then we talked about Jesus our Sanctifier.

Sanctification is a process, and it is a process that will last our lifetime. It is us choosing to grow spiritually in God's Word and in our walk with God by faith in the name of Jesus. This is us choosing to walk out our lives like the Person of Jesus, because of the saving grace of God by the sacrifice of Jesus our Savior.

Romans 6:23 says, "For the wages of sin is death…" And 1 John 3:8 (ESV) says, "Whoever makes a practice of sinning is of the devil, for the devil has been sinning from the beginning."

Jesus gave us the opportunity, with the help of the Holy Spirit, to choose a life set apart from the world and remove the spiritual blinders of the great tempter, the liar, the deceiver, the enemy: Satan.

Our friend demonstrated to us what a good character looks like; He lived a life worthy of legacy. Our friend is walking beside us, helping us through sanctification, and helping guide us to a good and worthy and holy life, set apart from the world, and toward those words, "Well done my good and faithful servant" (Matthew 25:21).

The Person of Jesus, our friend, is Jesus our Savior, who is also Jesus our Sanctifier.

Our Friend became Our Savior who is Our Sanctifier and who is the power from which we are granted the authority to heal.

Then we talked about Jesus our Healer.

Jesus "gave [us] authority to drive out impure spirits and to heal every disease and sickness" (Matthew 10:1).

Our Friend is our Savior and our Sanctifier in whom we have the authority to use His name to be Jesus our Healer.

Finally, we talked about Jesus our Coming King and Living Missionally.

We all live in one of two kingdoms: God's or the world's.

"...if anyone loves the world, love for the Father is not in him" (1 John 2:15). The ruler of this world is the devil (John 12:31; John 8:44-47; Matthew 4:8-9).

We must choose whose kingdom we will abide in, then we will truly know whom we call king.

"But if serving the Lord seems undesirable to you, then choose for yourselves this day whom you will serve...in whose land you are living. But as for me and my household, we will serve the Lord" (Joshua 24:15).

And how do we serve our King? How do we live missionally?

By choosing to give our life to God (Yahweh); by choosing to live in His kingdom; by choosing to live under the will of our King; by choosing to love Him who first loved us (1 John 4:19), and by sharing our King's good news to all whom He loves, which is all people—by spreading His Gospel, His love, His open invitation for saving grace and redemption, and by being his "witnesses…to the ends of the earth" (Acts 1:8), we will be servants of the one true King, and fulfill the calling of our Friend, our Savior, our Sanctifier, our Healer, our coming King.

Jesus said, "All authority in heaven and on earth has been given to me. Therefore go and make disciples of all nations, baptizing them in the name of the Father and of the Son and of the Holy Spirit, and teaching them to obey everything I have commanded you. And surely I am with you always, to the very end of the age" (Matthew 28:18-20).

That is living missionally.

Chapter 10:

Sinner's Prayer of Salvation

"Thank you, God, for your son Jesus Christ, forgiveness of my sins, and everlasting life."

Judy B. Jones[1]

If you have not yet accepted Jesus as your Lord and Savior and invited Him to live in your heart, then now is the time.

Believe in your heart, by faith, that Jesus died on the cross for your sins, that He rose again, that He lives and sits at the right hand of the Father (God), and that He is your King. As the Bible says in Romans 10:9-10, "If you declare with your mouth, 'Jesus is Lord,' and believe in your heart that God raised him from the dead, you will be saved. For it is with your heart that you believe and are justified, and it is with your mouth that you profess your faith and are saved."

Now is the time.

If you desire to be saved and have not yet made Jesus your King, then proclaim this prayer out loud and believe it in your heart:

Jesus, forgive me of my unbelief. I confess that you are my Lord and Savior, and I believe in my heart that God raised you from the dead. Lord, by faith in your Word, and through the confession of my own mouth, I invite you, Jesus, into my heart, and I receive salvation now. I thank you for dying on the cross for my sins, for taking my place, for being my advocate; I thank you for your saving grace, and I thank you for saving me. In Jesus name, amen.

Chapter 11:

Now What?

"Ask and it will be given to you; seek and you will find; knock and the door will be opened to you."

Matthew 7:7[1]

Now that you have learned more about "Who is Jesus," and you have hopefully been able to answer the question "Who do you say Jesus is," and taken the sinners prayer for salvation and accepted Jesus as your Lord and Savior, inviting Him into your heart, and beginning the sanctification process in your life, you are probably asking, "Now what?"

Now is the time to act.

As the parable is in Mark 4:1-9 and 4:14-20, "Again Jesus began to teach by the lake. The crowd that gathered around him was so large that he got into a boat and sat in it out on the lake, while all the people were along the shore at the water's edge. He taught them many things by parables, and in his teaching said: 'Listen! A farmer went out to sow his seed. As he was scattering the seed, some fell along the path, and the birds came and ate it up. Some fell on rocky places, where it did not have much soil. It sprang up quickly, because the soil was shallow. But when the sun came up, the plants were scorched, and they withered because they had no root. Other seed fell among thorns, which grew up and choked the plants, so that they did not bear grain. Still other seed fell on good soil. It came up, grew and produced a crop, some multiplying thirty, some sixty, some a hundred times.' Then Jesus said, 'Whoever has ears to hear, let them hear.'"

"'The farmer sows the word. Some people are like seed along the path, where the word is sown. As soon as they hear it, Satan comes and takes away the word that was sown in them. Others, like seed sown on rocky places, hear the word and at once receive it with joy. But since they have no root, they last only a short time. When trouble or persecution comes because of the word, they quickly fall away. Still others, like seed sown among thorns, hear the word; but the worries of this life, the deceitfulness of wealth and the desires for other things come in and choke the word, making it unfruitful. Others, like seed sown on good soil, hear the word, accept it, and produce a crop—some thirty, some sixty, some a hundred times what was sown.'"

Once that seed is firmly planted and you choose to water it, you have chosen to seek Jesus and defy Satan.

The Devil—Satan—will try to steal the message of God from your spirit, from your memory, from your thoughts. If Satan can stop the seed from being planted, drain it of nourishment, shade it from the light, strangle the roots, or corrupt the fruit from the inside, then he surely will try. Because once that seed is firmly planted and you choose to water it, then you have chosen to seek Jesus and defy Satan.

The Bible clearly says in Matthew 7:7, "Ask and it will be given to you; seek and you will find; knock and the door will be opened to you." And the Devil does not want you to ask or speak to God (prayer), seek Him and His Truth (reading the Bible and assembling with believers), or knock on the door (accept Jesus, attend church and be ministered to).

If you do not own a Bible yet, I highly suggest you go buy one. There are many translations out there, but the easiest translations to understand, for most, are the NIV (New International Version), the NLT (New Living Translation), and the NKJV (New King James Version).

The Old Testament was originally written in Hebrew and the New Testament was originally written in Greek. Because of this, Bibles are translated into English and every other language for people to read God's Word for themselves, and, in doing so, they must be transcribed, unless you can read Hebrew and Greek. Bible scholars spend copious amounts of time ensuring the translations are as accurate as possible; however, there are three types of translations to be aware of: Word-for-Word, Thought-for-Thought, and Paraphrase.

Word-for-Word is a direct Hebrew or Greek word translated (the best it can be) into modern language—in this case, my native language of English.

Thought-for-Thought is an examination of the whole sentence, or phrase, and translating it for the easiest reading. Here, their aim is the meaning of what was written, not the exact word for word.

Paraphrase is the restating of the original idea using the modern wording of the time it was translated. It's goal is to express the message in an easy-to-understand, more conversational way.

Thought-for-Thought and Paraphrase are typically the easiest to read because they are written more in modern language form to help the reader.

The translations go, as far as I understand it, in this order:

Word-for-Word translation

1. NASB (New American Standard Bible)

2. AMP (Amplified Bible)

3. ESV (English Standard Version)

4. RSV (Revised Standard Version)

5. KJV (King James Version)

6. NKJV (New King James Version)

Thought-for-Thought translation

7. NAB (New American Bible)

8. NJB (New Jerusalem Bible)

9. NIV (New International Version)

10. NLT (New Living Translation)

Paraphrase translation

11. GNT (Good News Translation)

12. CEV (Contemporary English Version)

13. TLB (The Living Bible)

14. MSG (The Message Bible)

You should begin reading your Bible, every day if possible. That is how you will get God's Word into you and renew your mind.

If you are not a part of a local church, then you should consider joining one. Find a church that is Christian based, believes in Jesus' death, burial and resurrection, and teaches the Truth of God's Word. There are some out there that, on the surface, look and sound like they are walking directly with God, but the more you read the Bible for yourself, the more you will be able to discern the Truth—many of these churches have strayed from God's Word and have instead compromised God's Word with the world; they deny what God clearly states (usually condemns) and imply that God made a mistake or was wrong in that area—this is what is known as false teachers or false prophets or false shepherds misleading God's people and they teach things contrary to God's Word. Also, find a church you are willing to get involved in and serve in, this will help you in your spiritual growth and help build connections with other believers.

Once you are in a church, you should seek to get baptized. Baptism is a sign to everyone and to God that you choose Him. "And Peter said to them, 'Repent and be baptized every one of you in the name of Jesus Christ for the forgiveness of your sins, and you will receive the gift of the Holy Spirit'" (Acts 2:38 ESV). Baptism is important and should not be overlooked.

Spend time each day in prayer with God. Remember, prayer is your communication channel with God. God is your friend; He wants to talk with you, guide you, and help you in life. If you are unsure how to pray, just talk—have a conversation with God as if you would any other friend. But do not forget to also listen. God sometimes speaks in the whispers, in a small still voice. He will also guide you through the Holy Spirit—that inner voice that tells you when something is right or wrong.

God never ignores the heart that truly reaches out for Him.

Make friends with other believers. "As iron sharpens iron, so one person sharpens another" (Proverbs 27:17).

Until you find a church home, you can view some great pastors and teachings online. Some of my favorite are (in no particular order): Ron Woods (at theAssembly.org), Justin Graves (at FoundationsChurch.tv), Robert Jeffress, Allen Jackson, Creflo Dollar, Joseph Prince, James Merritt, Beth Moore, and Jentezen Franklin.

Bibliography

Acknowledgment

1.   Proverbs 3:5-6

Chapter 1: Prologue

1.   "Zig Ziglar Quotes." BrainyQuote.com. BrainyMedia Inc, 2022. 9 April 2022. https://www.brainyquote.com/quotes/zig_ziglar_380874

Chapter 2: Introduction

1.   "John C. Maxwell Quotes." BrainyQuote.com. BrainyMedia Inc, 2022. 9 April 2022. https://www.brainyquote.com/quotes/john_c_maxwell_383606

2.   Story adapted from joke "Sure is hot down here"

Chapter 3: Who is Jesus?

1.   "Winston Churchill Quotes." BrainyQuote.com. BrainyMedia Inc, 2026. 7 January 2026. https://www.brainyquote.com/quotes/winston_churchill_111314

Chapter 4: Jesus the Person

1.   Jones, Josh C. *America: if you can keep it*. Broken Arrow, OK, FMS Books, 2025.

2.   Story adapted from a joke

3.   "Orson Welles Quotes." BrainyQuote.com. BrainyMedia Inc, 2022. 24 January 2022. https://www.brainyquote.com/quotes/orson_welles_142014

4.   "Ann Landers Quotes." BrainyQuote.com. BrainyMedia Inc, 2022. 24 January 2022. https://www.brainyquote.com/quotes/ann_landers_143025

5.   Jones, Josh C. *Destiny: Rich or Poor, Life or Death Choose Your Destiny*. Broken Arrow, OK, FMS Books, 2024.

Chapter 5: Jesus our Savior

1.   "Charles Spurgeon Quotes." BrainyQuote.com. BrainyMedia Inc, 2022. 8 February 2022. https://www.brainyquote.com/quotes/charles_spurgeon_718690

2.   Story adapted from a children's joke "God is missing. Where is God?"

3.   "Savior." *Merriam-Webster.com*. Merriam-Webster, 2021. Web. 8 February 2022.

4.   "Salvation." *Merriam-Webster.com*. Merriam-Webster, 2021. Web. 8 February 2022.

5.   The Bible Explains Dinosaurs. 2004. Hebron, KY

6.   Jones, Josh C. *From Blueprint to Reality: Hypothetical Foundations in Action*.

7.   Jones, Josh C. *Building Your Life Blueprint: Foundations for Lasting Success*.

8.   "Atonement." *Merriam-Webster.com*. Merriam-Webster, 2021. Web. 8 February 2022.

9.   Fisher, Sarah E. "Kippur: Atonement, Breaking the Barrier." *Hebrew Word Lessons*, 8 Sept. 2021, https://

hebrewwordlessons.com/2019/10/06/kippur-atonement-breaking-the-barrier/.

10.   George Orwell. *1984.* (New York, NY: New American Library, 1961).

11.   *Do You Believe?* Dir. Jon Gunn. Pure Flix Entertainment, 2015. Film.

Chapter 6: Jesus our Sanctifier

1.   "William Ames Quotes." BrainyQuote.com. BrainyMedia Inc, 2022. 12 February 2022. https://www.brainyquote.com/quotes/william_ames_301289

2.   Story adapted from a joke

3.   "Sanctify." *Merriam-Webster.com*. Merriam-Webster, 2021. Web. 8 February 2022.

4.   Jones, Josh C. *Destiny: Rich or Poor, Life or Death Choose Your Destiny*. Broken Arrow, OK, FMS Books, 2024.

5.   Noland, Robert. *Do You Believe? Experience the full power of the cross: 40-Day Devotional*. Racine, Wisconsin, BroadStreet Publishing Group, LLC, 2015.

Chapter 7: Jesus our Healer

1.   Carpenter, Cindy. *Miracles Now*. Tustin, CA, Trilogy Christian Publishers, 2019.

2.   Story adapted from a joke

Chapter 8: Jesus our coming King & Living

Missionally

1.   "James Monroe Quotes." BrainyQuote.com. BrainyMedia Inc, 2022. 8 March 2022. https://www.brainyquote.com/quotes/james_monroe_789678

2.   Jones, Josh C. *Entrepreneur: Road Map For Success*. Tulsa, OK, Bush Publishing and Associates, LLC, 2021.

3.   Jones, Josh C. *Entrepreneur: Road Map For Success*. Tulsa, OK, Bush Publishing and Associates, LLC, 2021.

4.   Story adapted from a joke

Chapter 9: Conclusion

1.   The Holy Bible, New International Version. Grand Rapids: Zondervan House, 1984. Print.

a.   Genesis 2:17

2.   Yancey, Philip. *Disappointment With God: Three Questions No One Asks Aloud*. Grand Rapids, Michigan, Zondervan; New edition, 1997.

Chapter 10: Sinner's Prayer of Salvation

1.   Quote by Judy B. Jones

Chapter 11: Now What?

1.   The Holy Bible, New International Version. Grand Rapids: Zondervan House, 1984. Print.

a.   Matthew 7:7

About the Author

Josh C. Jones

Josh has a passion to help bring the truth, better understanding, hope, and entertainment to people through his writing and creativity. He hopes to change the perspective for a better understanding. Josh likes to laugh, which means he has emotions. Emotions mean he is human. Being human, he has experienced the ups and downs and the joys and pains of this life, just like everyone else. Through all this, he has chosen to write what he has learned in the hopes of helping others and igniting that spark to learn more, achieve more, and understand more.

Josh's journey thus far has taken him through creative fields, classrooms, studios, stages, and more, giving him a different perspective on people, purpose, and the power of truth. He approaches every project—whether writing, teaching, or speaking—with the belief that clarity and understanding can change a life. His work blends storytelling, reflection, philosophy, logic, and insight, shaped by a desire to help others think deeper, grow stronger, achieve more, and live life with purpose and intention.

Grounded in faith, curiosity, some sarcasm, and a genuine love for learning, Josh continues to examine the questions that do help shape our culture, our character, and our destiny. He invites readers to join him in that pursuit—to challenge assumptions, acquire knowledge, seek wisdom, and discover the strength that comes from building a life on purpose and truth.

You can visit his website at the following address,

www.JoshCJonesAuthor.com, where you can contact him, read more, view more, hear more, and see his published work.

Other Books by Josh C. Jones

DESTINY: Rich or Poor, Life or Death, Choose Your Destiny

Your future isn't fate—it's a choice. This bold, inspiring guide shows you how to break free from circumstance, claim your power, and create a life worth living. Will you rise to the challenge? The choice is yours. Get the book and claim your destiny—starting now!

ENTREPRENEUR: Road Map For Success

What if entrepreneurship was not just about business, but about mastering your life? This bold, inspiring guide redefines "entrepreneur" as a mindset—one that builds character, purpose, and resilience. It's a roadmap to success, respect, and fulfillment. Will you rise to the challenge and become the entrepreneur of your life?

Building Your Life Blueprint: Foundations for Lasting Success

What Are You Building Your Life On?

Every belief, decision, and action is laid upon a foundation—but is yours solid or shifting? In this eye-opening and soul-stirring book, you're invited to examine the ground beneath your feet and the principles guiding your path. With timeless wisdom and piercing questions, it challenges you to seek clarity, live with conviction, and build a life of purpose and strength in a world full of noise and uncertainty. The journey to a meaningful life begins with one choice: your foundation.

From Blueprint to Reality: Hypothetical Foundations in Action

Will You Stand When It Counts?

Life doesn't pause, and neither does pressure. In *From Blueprint to Reality: Hypothetical Foundations in Action*, you're challenged not just to believe—but to live what you believe. Building on the principles of *Building Your Life Blueprint*, this powerful follow-up dares you to apply conviction in a world that constantly pushes for compromise. When life tests your values, will you rise with strength or waver in the storm?

AMERICA: If You Can Keep It (Finalist, *WriterCon 2025*)

What if the greatest threat to American liberty came not from outside, but from within? This urgent, passionate call to action warns of a slow decay—ignorance, complacency, and distortion of truth—and inspires readers to reclaim the founding ideals that shaped a nation. Will you rise to defend it?

AMERICA: Then and Now, a poem by Josh C. Jones (Award Winning Poem.)

AMERICA: Then and Now isn't just a nod to literary acclaim, it's a poetic reckoning with the soul of America. This bold and reflective work blends political insight with philosophical depth, using powerful metaphor and lyrical language to explore how far the nation may have strayed from its roots.

AMERICA: Then and Now is not a celebration of trophies but a solemn, stirring commentary on what we risk losing when we forget who we are. For readers who appreciate thoughtful verse with a message—and who aren't afraid to wrestle with uncomfortable truths—this poetic book offers both beauty and a call to conscience.

Making sense of America's newest Guild... Again: What I discovered in my search for answers.

What if "MAGA" was not the end of the conversation, but the beginning? This bold, thought provoking book challenges assumptions, sparks dialogue, and inspires understanding across divides. If you're tired of echo chambers and hungry for deeper conversations, this is your invitation.

Read it and rethink what it means to listen.

The Tilted Scales: Let Truth Arise.

A poetic examination of modern America—its divisions, distortions, and forgotten ideals. Through powerful verse, vivid imagery, and a blend of social commentary, historical reflection, and scriptural wisdom, it confronts cultural hypocrisy, shifting standards of justice, and the growing tension between truth and emotion. Challenging readers to question the narratives they're told, the history they forget, and the divisions they quietly accept, this collection is both convicting and hopeful, calling its audience to honesty, courage, and balance—to let truth arise where confusion and division have taken root.

TRUTH: A Courageous Journey to Discover the Truth That Will Never Fail You.

A reflective and Scripture-rooted exploration of truth, this book invites readers to examine the foundations of their beliefs and the convictions that shape their lives. Through stories, insight, and honest questions, it guides seekers toward the unchanging Truth that brings clarity, strength, and lasting peace. It's a call to build a life that can withstand every storm by standing firmly on what is absolute and eternal.

Special Note

Please remember that if you like a book or an author's work, the best thing you can do to help the message, story, or author is to tell others. You can also do this by leaving reviews and/or ratings on the online site where you purchased the material. By doing so, you help the book and/or author gain more exposure and reach more people. This is something that not all authors will express publicly, but all authors do hope the reader will graciously do, and we are appreciative and grateful for it.

Thank you.

—Josh C. Jones
joshcjonesauthor.com

www.ingramcontent.com/pod-product-compliance
Lightning Source LLC
Chambersburg PA
CBHW051413050726

47595CB00010B/4043